POINT LAST SEEN

BEACON PRESS
BOSTON

POINT LAST SEEN

A WOMAN TRACKER'S STORY

HANNAH NYALA

BEACON PRESS
25 Beacon Street
Boston, Massachusetts 02108-2892

BEACON PRESS BOOKS
are published under the auspices of
the Unitarian Universalist Association of Congregations.

To protect the identities of everyone mentioned in this book,
all names and dates, as well as many locations, have been changed.

03 02 01 00 99 98 97   8 7 6 5 4 3 2 1

Text design by Anne Chalmers
Composition by Wilsted & Taylor

Library of Congress Cataloging-in-Publication Data
Nyala, Hannah.
   Point last seen : a woman tracker's story / Hannah Nyala.
      p.   cm.
   ISBN 0-8070-7092-0
1. Footprints—United States—Identification.   2. Tracking and trailing—
United States.   3. Missing persons—Investigation—United States.   4. Family
violence—United States.   I. Title.
HV8077.5.F6N93   1997
363.2′562—dc20
[B]   96-18397

FOR MY SON AND DAUGHTER.

*Writing is an act of utmost faith—and hope—
that your lives will never again be marked by
the violence of our past.*

*And in memory of Samson (1986–1995),
dear friend and companion.*

CONTENTS

SEARCHER'S BRIEFING

SOME PEOPLE walk with both eyes focused on their goal: the highest mountain peak in the range, the fifty-mile marker, the finish line. They stay motivated by anticipating the end of the journey. Since I tend to be easily distracted, I travel somewhat differently—one step at a time, with many pauses in between.

Occasionally the pauses become full stops that can last anywhere from two minutes to ten hours. More often they're less definite, a few extra seconds spent lingering over the sight of a dainty wildflower growing out of a rock wall or a feisty beetle hurrying along, the sound of a cactus wren's boisterous song or a rattler's warning buzz, the feel of a warm wind slipping past. Invariably my eyes are drawn to the ground, to the many intricate signs littering its surface. Any one set of these marks tells a story—of existence, connections, relationships, of life lived mostly at the edges of human awareness. The almost imperceptible trail a scorpion leaves behind often means nothing to the humans who tower over—and never see—it. Yet let one of us plop down on the end of that trail unknowingly, and what we did not think to see before will be brought sharply to our attention. Even then most of us would only look for and see the offending stinger, the scorpion itself, and not the signs which could have forewarned us of the nonhuman reality we were about to encounter.

Seldom do humans actually sit on something as memorable as a scorpion. We are far more likely to settle ourselves down on much tinier, less potent creatures, who cannot retalitate enough to break into our oblivion with a sting. Then we get up and go on our way, never having noticed them or the tracks that could have led us into a larger world. Trapped by our concepts and languages and the utter predictability of our five senses, we often forget to wonder what we're missing as we hurry along toward goals we may not even have chosen.

I became a tracker by default, not design, when my tendency to be distracted by life's smallest signs grew into an unrelenting passion to trace those obscure, often puzzling patterns somewhere, *any*where—to their source or end or simply to some midpoint in between. But when I began tracking lost people, what had begun as an eccentric habit—following footprints on the ground—quickly matured into an avocation. Reining in and focusing my gaze, I routinely walked and looked at tracks for hours on end, not for relaxation, enlightenment, food, or in fact for any of the reasons people normally walk through the natural environment. I now commonly walk toward a single goal: to meet the person at the other end of the tracks.

My training has a perverse set of origins: an early childhood dedicated to thwarting the efforts of hunters in the Mississippi woods; a young adulthood spent trying to escape and then hide from an abusive husband, a time when tracks on the ground functioned as an early warning signal for my two children and me; and a stint working with a search-and-rescue unit in the National Park Service. But time, perhaps fortunately for the human species, displays an uncanny genius for jostling us loose from our origins.

A few years ago, with a sociocultural anthropology degree in hand, I went to Africa to study tracking in a society where men are renowned for their tracking abilities. What my children and I learned there shook the foundations of our already unsteady world. This book is a set of stories about my journey as a tracker, about how tracking, the deceptively simple act of following footprints on the ground, opens a window between the human soul and its natural environment, encouraging humility and understanding. These stories are also about the linkages tracking forges between one human soul and another. However tenuous and unarticulated they may be, the ties between the tracker and the person up ahead constitute the very heart of tracking. Without fail, following someone else's footprints always forces me to walk alongside them long enough to rethink the most perverse of my origins. As we track, we too are being tracked.

Trackers move through the natural environment for specific reasons. What we find—what we even look for in the first place—is profoundly shaped by culture, by the collective memories of our societies, and by our own experiences. My tracking is deeply influenced not just by having grown up on a small farm in Mississippi or by having learned to follow the footprints of lost people through the Mojave Desert, but also by having been, for many years, a tracked woman. Ending an abusive marriage sometimes exacts a terrible price. After seven years of being beaten by my first husband, I took my two children and ran. We hid, were found and threatened, managed to escape and hide again, but all our hiding places were quickly discovered, and fear marked our every move, both before and after my children were taken from me.

Nothing can adequately prepare a human for becoming another's prey. The hunted person quickly realizes that survival is anything but instinctive, and is utterly reversible. In subtle ways, being hunted down changes your givens forever: You soon learn that details matter enormously as you become alert in ways you could never have imagined. You no longer expect truth to emerge from life's niceties, so you begin to perceive people as many-layered, often paradoxical actors. You know that when violence erupts, many individuals of your species will disappear rapidly, leaving you to face the brutality alone. Every single thing you once trusted or wanted to believe about human society disintegrates. And even when you reach a place of apparent safety, you can never forget the terror from which you've come or explain it away with rationale or common sense, idealism or selective remembering. Once you've been hunted, you know that there is no such thing as "safe."

This book is about tracking, not domestic violence. Yet the

two are intricately interwoven in my existence. Tracking marks my continued search for a safe place, while violence marks my repeated encounters with fear. Neither has yet canceled the other out.

Trackers make connections between what they see on the ground and everything they know or feel or suspect about those physical signs. Although novices often start out with their eyes focused somewhere near their feet—in search and rescue we were taught not to move ahead from one track until the next one had been found—they gradually begin to look farther ahead of themselves, moving faster and more confidently in the process. In the Kalahari, Ju/Wasi and !Kung Bushmen sometimes track at a run with their eyes scanning the ground about fifteen feet in front of them, regularly checking the earth passing under their feet to confirm their distance vision. When I tried that the first few times, especially in the dense Kalahari vegetation, I faithfully lost the track every time: Whenever I started running, my eyes would bob up and down right along with my feet, making any tracks blur into nearby bushes, losing all connection with the trail. For weeks I tried to run and track, but ended every attempt defeated after a few yards. Fortunately, for trackers, consistent failures can often be more instructive than successes. Only after learning to perceive both space and signs differently did I begin to move with the tracks, to learn to come alongside in ways I had never been able to do as a search-and-rescue tracker.

Some trackers claim to have the ability to get inside the head of the person or animal they are tracking. Citing the legendary skills of people like the Bushmen, their goal is to emulate those legends, to see through the eyes of the hunted animal or to think through the mind of the lost person. Perhaps contrarily, I have always had trouble with the whole concept of getting inside anyone else's head for any reason—especially into the mind of a lost person, who, after all, is confused enough for both of us. To find someone who is lost, I need the best of my own mind, my own ability to reason. Therefore, I try to walk alongside the person I am seeking, to understand and feel without losing my own ability to act capably. In both the Kalahari and the Namib Desert of southern Africa, I found people who helped me learn how to do that better—to walk alongside others (human or otherwise) not simply in tracking situations, but in life more generally.

Read these stories like a tracker: with your eyes on the ground and the horizon simultaneously. Pick up whatever information you can and keep it close at hand—don't filter out the extraneous, but don't get sidetracked by it either. Trackers can never know for sure that the clues they have are the best or most appropriate for the moment; instead they can only operate on a series of best guesses, trusting both intuition and knowledge, yet at the same time heartily doubting both. Discover any connections, but draw your own conclusions about them in the end, for only you can decide whether they are valid for your search.

CUTTING FOR SIGN

MAY 1987

JOSHUA TREE NATIONAL MONUMENT

When the park radio beckoned a while ago, I was stretched out in the backyard hammock eating a bowl of fresh strawberries, reading a pleasantly unchallenging book, and planning to spend the rest of the day doing little else. But five minutes after the ranger's voice crackled over that box, I was throwing a search pack into the back seat of my car—and the hammock is probably still swinging my book to sleep under the palo verde tree as I drive toward the staging area for the search already underway. Probably should've put the book inside the house, but can't go back to do it now. Oh well, this is the desert—the book could sit there for three years and not get rained on, so it'll probably survive a night or two. With any luck I might be back before dark anyway. On searches, though, the return home is impossible to predict. Today there's a sixty-five-year-old woman lost in the Cottonwood area—that's all the information I got over the radio—so we could be finished in two hours or stay out for the next two weeks. At this point I wouldn't be willing to bet a dime either way. So much for relaxation.

The Cottonwood Visitor Center is crowded, as usual this time of year—spring's flowers lure visitors from all over the world— so I park and wend my way through clumps of tourists who have no idea that one of their fellow humans just took off down a trail and didn't come back. But the back office is a different story, because everyone here knows there's a problem: the agitated young man clenching and unclenching his hands and repeating over and over, "But when she left us you could still practically *see* the parking lot!" and his wife, trying to pat her husband on the shoulder every few seconds (hard to do when somebody's pacing, even if it is in a six-foot-square space); Alan, the campground volunteer, shaking his head in empathy, and his wife, Rita, manning the crackling radio; and the district ranger, finishing the initial lost persons report, his voice even and professional as he questions the pacing man and his patting wife. I know this ranger—married him just a few months ago, in fact— so I can tell that he's starting to get knots in his stomach now, just as I am. There is something about facing a flesh-and-blood person who has lost another just-as-real person that sweeps away the comfortable "careless tourist" stereotype we often use to survive living and working inside a National Park: Seeing people who have lost one dear to them yanks knots inside me as quick as anything can. Frank, Alan, Rita, and I all feel tense, but there's no need for these two frightened people to know that The best thing we can do for them and their grandmother is to do our jobs well; that sounds corny, but it is nevertheless entirely true.

I get both an introduction and a welcome; the presence of a tracker often helps convince scared family members that the Park Service does know how to conduct a search—and does intend to do something more than just ask pages of questions. Those questions are critical, though, to what I'm about to do, and as I glance over his shoulder at the report, Frank briefs me.

"She's sixty-five, a strong hiker, in pretty good health except for a blood sugar problem, got tired of hiking so decided to return to the campsite while the rest of the family went on. She's been out now for four hours, has only a small canteen and no overnight gear, was last seen on the Lost Palms Trail about a quarter mile from the oasis."

"Shoes?"

"I haven't finished the report yet," Frank says, and we both turn to the pacing man—the lost hiker's grandson, Joe Jessons.

"What kind of shoes is she wearing, Joe?" I ask.

He can't remember, but his wife, Helen, does: "They're hiking boots and she's a size eight."

Joe stops pacing long enough to register surprise. "How do you know that?"

"Well, I was with Grandma when she bought them last year and she was saying just this morning that she needed a new pair."

"Do you remember the brand?" I ask.

"Oh yes, they're High Tecs—like yours," Helen says, pointing at my feet, "only low-cut."

Helen is pleased with herself, Joe returns to his pacing, and I pretend to be happy with the information. But in reality, the knots inside both Frank and me just cinched themselves a few notches tighter: Mrs. Jessons happens to be wearing one of the more popular hiking boots in the state right now, and there's no telling how many size eights went wandering around Lost Palms Trail in the last few hours. Mine have a distinctive bullet-shaped notch cut in both heels to identify me as a tracker (not lost). Ruby Jessons' shoes, like every other pair out there today, won't be notched—her soles will be straight from the factory. But Helen's information is a start. At least Mrs. Jessons' shoes are a year old—that means they may have signs of wear as distinctive as my notches.

The briefing is about to take a serious turn, so Alan suggests that Joe and Helen come outside and have a drink of water before finishing the report. They go, looking glad to be reminded that they're thirsty, and pleased to be out of the tiny room and momentarily distracted.

"So they've been all through the campground then? No signs that she ever got back?" I ask. Frank nods. "Then the best guess is that she's off trail somewhere?" Another nod, so I look at the topographic map on the wall. "If she's still moving, she could be miles from here by now."

"Yeah that's what it looks like," Frank replies. "Listen, I've got Riverside on standby—do you want me to bring them in?"

he asks, referring to the tracking unit I prefer to work with above all others.

"She's been out for four hours?" I ask, reading from the report. "We've only got three hours 'til dark. I think we need to pull out the stops on this one—can Danny fly the trackers in?"

"They've got two rock rescues going on topside now," Frank says. "So we may have trouble getting a chopper down here for a while—but I'll see what we can do. Would you head down to the PLS [point last seen] and report back on what you turn up?" he asks without waiting for a response, already turning toward the radio to begin mobilizing search-and-rescue (SAR) resources. I reply over my shoulder, "On my way."

"Oh Hannah," Frank calls out, "We may need to move the search base over to the house—okay by you?"

"Sure, no problem," I say, thinking that had I known this was coming, I'd have done my laundry instead of reading all morning. Not that it matters much: Whenever we base a search from the house, there are so many people and things going every direction that probably no one notices the state of my laundry.

The clumps of tourists out front have gotten wind of the search now and are forming into larger groups of curious, concerned people. Strapping on my chest harness and fastening in a mobile radio, I walk over to Joe and Helen and say in my most reassuring, confident tone, "Now listen, I know you're worried—she's your grandmother—but we're *going* to find her, so you just hang in here, okay? We'll keep you informed, won't we, Alan?"

Alan nods and smiles, says, "We sure will," and Helen seems reassured, but Joe doesn't. "I'll go with you," he says to me, brushing off his wife's arm.

"Oh no—that wouldn't work at all. Frank needs you to finish that report, and besides, I'm going to be moving fast."

"I can keep up and she," he says, nodding toward Helen, "can finish the report."

Choosing my words carefully, I say, "Listen Joe, I'm a tracker and the best chance your grandmother has is for us to find her tracks quickly. The fewer footprints out there the better, the *easier* my job is. There are already a lot of people wearing hiking boots—including me—but mine are marked, see?" I raise one foot so he can see how the tread has been altered. "You can help best—in fact, all of you can help [this to the gathering crowd] by staying *out* of the search areas completely, okay?"

This pragmatic bit of information seems to have a settling effect on the young man; perhaps the sight of my shoe tread helps convince him that I have done this before. Joe smiles briefly and returns to pacing again, tightening the knots in my stomach, and I head for Cottonwood Springs.

During the spring, the Lost Palms Oasis trail probably has several hundred feet on it every weekend, though few people hike the full distance. Most, like Mrs. Jessons, get tired and turn around before the halfway mark. Some don't even get that far, stopping instead to look at the old mining arrastra. Children, less in awe of history than adults, make good use of the circular remains, jumping, stepping, and crawling over and on and through them. Some hikers abandon the trail to sit on the rocks that flank the spring and watch the birds, while others wander down into the wash and pick wildflowers or feed the ground squirrels (neither activity is legal here). All in their own way are enjoying their National Park experience, staying close to the trailhead, which is just about to be closed because of the ongoing search. Alan should be here in a few minutes to do the honors for the people who are milling around, possibly thinking about hiking the trail. He'll explain the situation, some of them will grumble, and he'll suggest alternative walks, which some of them will take. Those who had already decided not to hike the trail will probably be thankful they didn't and that they (and their grandmothers) are thus safe.

But some visitors have long since continued past the spring, following the trail I'm now on toward an even more isolated desert oasis. These people—their footprints, actually—are what concern me now. I said they follow the trail, and strictly speaking this is true. But even more pertinent for my purposes is an opposing truth: Most of these hikers "follow" the trail in only the most vague sense of the verb. They get off the path regularly, taking short side trips to inspect a cactus bloom or a chuckwalla, to photograph themselves or an especially appealing pile of rocks, to rest before starting up the next hill, or to relieve themselves. Because Mrs. Jessons's footprints might be mixed up with anyone else's, I can't afford to misread these sidetrip tracks. I work parallel to the trail, seven or eight yards from it—we call this strategy "cutting for sign." Sign cutting operates on a couple of basic assumptions: For one thing, few of the side trips made by most visitors ever bring them this far off the trail, so there are fewer prints to work through; for another, if Mrs. Jessons left this area, I'm assuming she went on foot, which means that I should find her tracks in the sign cut on one side or the other of this trail. I'll work the side nearest the campground first, since I know she was heading there and can reasonably infer that she may have decided to take a shortcut.

The going is rough in places, steep and rocky on this side of the trail. I find more tracks than I'd expected. A few people had several beers and an illegal campfire out here a couple of nights ago, leaving a used condom behind; two people were exceptionally modest, judging by how far off the trail they went in order to urinate; and one kid managed to get almost thirty feet off the trail before a concerned adult caught up with him and carried him back to the trail. I say "him," even though I really have no idea whether the kid was a boy or girl—the behavior gives no clue (girls can hie off just as quickly as boys) and neither do the shoes (waffle soles don't hint at gender). Compared to the trail, though, out here the traffic is light, and I move quickly, staying on the easiest tracking surfaces (sandy dirt or light gravel) when possible, taking my own side trips when a possible size eight shows up: one set of Adidas running shoes, two pairs of Nikes, and one pair of Birkenstocks. There are quite a few lug-soled boots out here, but most of them are way too large to belong to a woman who's only 5′4″ and 120 pounds. I see no prints that could pass for High Tecs but my own and one pair of size fives. So much for my earlier worries about the most popular hiking boot problem. As I encounter each set of possible prints, I draw a circle around them and tie a small piece of orange flagging to the nearest bush—just in case Helen was wrong about the brand and we need to follow up on any of these tracks later. I even mark the size fives, figuring it can't hurt to know where they are. For now, after radioing the information in to search base, I will continue to look for size eight High Tecs (but will ask Frank to have someone query Helen again, just in case).

Could Helen have been mistaken about her grandmother's shoes? That question looms larger as I cross over the trail, well beyond the point where Mrs. Jessons turned back, to start working the other side. But then the radio crackles and Frank says to go with the High Tec eights. Clearly Helen is sure about this, so for now I'll flag, mark, and leave everything else, a luxury trackers seldom have in searches since there are very few Helens in the world of lost people—most of us, myself included a few years ago, wouldn't have noticed such a trivial detail even if our grandmothers had started out the day barefoot.

On this side of the trail, much of which heads downhill, even more side trips are evident. One bunch of purple lupine has attracted no less than six photographers, probably because it is photogenically growing out of a crack in a vertical rock wall. And somebody stepped off the trail into soft dirt that gave way   and wound up sitting on his or her backside about six feet below the trail a few seconds later, narrowly missing the spines of a yucca. Oh, here's the kid from the other side, making another trip off trail, gender revealed (girls can't stand in one spot and pee eighteen inches in front of themselves). Not ten feet further and I find what I'm looking for: a pair of size eight High Tecs heading down the hill. Mrs. Jessons. Joe and Helen's Grandma. It's got to be her. God, let it be her, I think, while radioing my location in to base and once again marking the spot, but this time with orange and blue flagging. The nearest trackers are at least three hours away, so Frank tells me to carry on solo   not the best search tactic, but one we'll have to use for now. Grandma Jessons has too big a head start on us.

Mentally, I have taken the tracker's step forward: Now that I have connected with her footprints, Mrs. Jessons is "Grandma" to me too. For an unspecified part of the immediate future, I must get as close to Joe and Helen's grandmother as possible, must know her as intimately as I can, and fictive kin terms work as well as anything to help me establish cognitive proximity. I'm not getting inside Grandma's head here, nor am I trying to, but by using an informal, even affectionate form of address I make her seem more real to me and create a conceptual bond with the lost stranger. Nor is the affection feigned. Searching for someone means I care deeply, intensely for them. Kin terms simply help me express that emotion without undermining my ability to do what I need to.

Grandma has headed down a natural drainage that the poetically inclined would describe as a tiny canyon. What is most relevant about this feature now is the fact that it eventually crosses the Monument's main road. Before I even finish knotting the flagging, Frank has dispatched Alan to the road; before Al has had time to reach his truck I'm a good city block down the drainage, tracking Grandma as fast as I can see and trot. I'm staying a couple feet to the right of her prints so as not to destroy them— I may lose her and have to come back and restart the track, and that would be harder to do if I've trampled all over her signs.

Grandma takes a sudden turn up a hill, leaving the drainage (so much for SAR theories that old people and children are most likely to take the path of least resistance), and I follow, attempting to figure out what on earth she is looking for. Oh, she came up here to look at this blooming brittle bush—she apparently doesn't know she's lost yet. We take a circuitous route past several flowering plants and one newly smashed barrel cactus— the bighorn sheep must've been here this morning—back down into the drainage, and continue moving toward the road. Alan's down there now, driving slowly back and forth, reporting to base that he sees no one yet. Too bad we don't have another tracker to cut for sign on the road. The temperature will drop fifteen degrees by sundown, and Grandma's not carrying a sweater. The knots tighten. I move faster. Up the right bank we go to inspect a rock fissure (Grandma probably saw a lizard up here), all the way to the top to look at a clump of mistletoe (maybe there was a shiny black phainopepla perched here when she came by), then drop partially down into the next drainage before circling around and crossing back into the first one. Suddenly, crossing a short rocky section, Grandma disappears, and I come to a screeching halt myself, sending tiny rocks skittering over the flat surface.

Where did she go? People can't fly, but if I didn't know better I'd say Grandma levitated herself out of here. Looking ahead, eyes shaded, to where the rocks give way to sandy dirt again, I see human tracks—but not Grandma's. By now I know her stride, the slightly turned right shoe, the soles worn down along the outsides of each track, the way she tends to drag that left foot whenever she's going uphill—wherever she went, she didn't go down this wash. Time for me to move again. Another fast perimeter cut—this time in a 360-degree circle around the rocky area—brings me alongside Grandma's tracks once more. She's headed up another side hill—no, she's going back down—well, maybe not. We are both now headed up the hill, and it seems that for the first time Grandma may be a little disoriented. At the top of the rise, she pauses and looks around (clearly a seasoned hiker, trying to reorient herself), takes a few steps forward, then stops and turns around. You've been too busy looking at flowers, Grandma, to recognize any of these landmarks behind you now, so why don't you sit down for a while and let me catch up with you?

That's exactly what she does next—sits down, digs her heels into the hillside, and taps her fingers on the ground beside her— but then obviously decides that waiting a few hours isn't the best use of her energy because she starts moving again, this time heading down into a different drainage. Getting set to go with her, I radio my location to search base from the hilltop (radio reception is poor to nonexistent from the wash bottoms here) and start off once again. Grandma's not looking at the flowers anymore, and she's probably moving faster, but she's winding around a lot, looking in every direction for something, anything, familiar. She is, in fact, doing the most natural—and the very worst—thing for a lost person to do: She's moving.

And she's no longer picking her routes so carefully either, I think, stumbling and sliding down a steep incline after her (at this rate she'll be lucky not to have me find her with a broken leg or something around the next bend, and I'll be lucky not to have broken my neck getting there). Suddenly my mental grouch session is interrupted by the sputter of the radio in my chest harness. It's Alan on local, coming through loud and clear (he can't be more than a quarter mile to the southwest now), saying, "They've got Mrs. Jessons at the VC [visitor center], Hannah, do you read?"

"All *right*, Al! Is she okay?" (On the local channel we use plain English and save the technical radio jargon for parkwide communications.)

"Yep, other than being thirsty and tired, she's in good shape. She came out onto the road about fifteen minutes ago and caught a ride up with some folks, missed me completely, but at least she got in all right."

Alan signs off, heading back to the VC, promising to sign me out with Frank, while I sit down to empty the sand and small stones out of my boots. One more live one at Cottonwood. We're setting records here these days—no dead lost people in over a year now. In the fading daylight I decide to work backward to the springs, removing the flagging I tied out on the way down and checking the route to see what else I can learn from it.

Moving slowly, feeling the tension leaving my body, I turn

back toward the trail Grandma and I have made. On reaching the rocky spot that stumped me earlier, I drop my pack and get down on hands and knees, and then stare at that stretch of ground from every conceivable angle until I finally convince myself that I can see where Grandma crossed it. Lying flat on my back, I drink from my water bottle without bothering about the tepid water that trickles down my neck and shirt collar. My bright yellow SAR shirt will go straight in the laundry tonight anyway. By now the sun is starting to set, and my knots have become small bumps of unexpended energy evenly distributed throughout my body: running will help. I backtrack Grandma and me at high speed (it's fairly easy to see footprints when you helped to make them yourself and were paying attention at the time), pausing only to remove the flagging I tied out on the way down. Soon after I reach the Lost Palms Trail I slow down to a walk, abruptly winded, just in time to see Frank coming toward me, wearing civvies—t-shirt, shorts, and running shoes. He's working his tension out too. Seeing me, he waves and grins and comes alongside to say, "Hey, want to go for a run? I can wait while you go change."

"Not a chance! Unlike you upper management types, I have been running all afternoon!"

Frank continues down the trail and I resume my backtracking, thinking how good it is finally to be married to a man who never shows the slightest desire to hit anyone. Pulling the last piece of flagging off a creosote bush, I head home with rubbery knees. Curious, isn't it—this tracking business? For the last few hours I have walked closely alongside a woman's footprints, helping lay a second set of size eight prints on the same trail, and now she's gone without my ever having laid eyes on her. We shared a path for a few hours and never met, but neither of us will soon forget this afternoon.

Two women heading home. One safe with her grandson and his wife. The other safe with her laundry.

AUGUST 1977
Kevin quoted the bible to me again today.

The parts about wives being submissive to their husbands and turning the other cheek. And then he hit me hard on the right side of my face with his open hand and yelled, "Now what are you supposed to do—or have you forgotten already, bitch?!"

Slowly I turned my head—and he hit my left cheek twice, fast and very hard.

"That's one for good measure, whore," he said angrily, turning away, then quickly back again. Grabbing my arms he threw me backward into the refrigerator, slamming my whole body up against it once, twice, three times, and then I lost count.

I don't remember the next part, only that I woke up on the floor with Kevin standing over me, holding his glass of iced tea and pointing first at it, then at me.

"Now the *next* time you serve *me* iced tea, you had better remember this: You're supposed to put in *six* ice cubes—that's SIX, not four, not seven, not five and one broken one—SIX ice cubes and ONLY SIX. That's the way I like it and that's the way you will fix it 'til the day you die—got that, idiot bitch?"

I nodded.

Kevin raised his arm high and threw the glass of iced tea hard at the tiled floor, then walked into the living room and picked up the laundry basket of clothes I'd just finished folding before he came in to dinner. Carrying them back into the kitchen, stomping so hard the whole trailer shook, he turned the basket upside down in midair, dumping all the clothes onto the wet floor. Kicking them around with one foot, he said coldly, "I'm going out for a few hours—you'd better have this mess cleaned up before I get back here!"

His truck roared away, and when the sound had gone with it, I got up and put the laundry back into the basket, picked up the broken glass and the ice cubes—seven of them melting fast into perfect puddles—and mopped the floor. Neither of us had taken even a bite of dinner, so I dished the food back into its bowls and set it on the stove. Only when I started the washing machine did I realize there was moisture on my face and lower lip. Not tears: I don't cry anymore. It was iced tea mixed with blood, dripping down the left side of my face, falling into the soapy water, and sinking beneath the bubbles with no sound and hardly a trace.

"And whosoever shall smite thee on thy right cheek, turn to him the other also." I didn't know this was how marriage would be. Leaning over the washing machine I wiped my face off with one of the tea-stained towels and tried to ignore the bitter nausea rising into my throat. Inside my stomach my baby shifted around slightly, a good reminder that I needed to work harder at being a better wife—and mother: somebody else was already depending on me. SIX ice cubes. I vowed not to forget again.

That night Kevin returned, quiet and remorseful. "I'm so sorry," he said, holding me close and flinching when he caught sight of the bruised skin behind my ear. "Are you all right?"

I nodded, not knowing what to say.

"I promise never to hurt you again—can you forgive me for this?" he said.

"Yes," I nodded, and felt Kevin exhale deeply. He was very sad to have hurt me—and relieved to know I was all right.

"I love you so much—do you still love me?" he asked, holding me away to look into my eyes.

I nodded again. He still loved me. Things would work out. They had to.

Sometimes love reverses itself so subtly and swiftly that its principals go on living, entirely unaware of the reversal until years later. Few emotions have love's ability to chain people into tightly interlocked cycles of joy and anger, laughter and silence, desperation and intense hope. I have repeatedly been asked, "But weren't there any warning signals before you married Kevin?"

The answer is yes, of course. But as a teenager, I had no language or concepts, no analytical frame whatsoever in which to sort out potentially abusive behaviors. I had only ideals and hopes and dreams back then. The rest had to be learned along the way.

AUGUST 1976

He seemed lonely. Quiet and sensitive. Standing on the edge of the group of young people after the morning's church service, Kevin was an auburn-haired, handsome young man of medium height. Tastefully dressed, he walked up to me and said with a friendly smile, "I like to hear you talk." My southern accent apparently was even noticeable in Missouri, where my parents had sent us that summer to attend a camp meeting.

Later that afternoon, over pizza, Kevin and I had a heated debate about the philosophy of predestination, and I left the local Pizza Hut assuming I would never see Kevin Myles again. But at dusk, he reappeared with a piece of paper in his hand.

"Not many people are intelligent enough or have enough nerve to argue with me," he said, adding, "I wrote something for you."

It was a poem about a young woman who suddenly walked into a lonely man's life and brought him an unexpected joy and a love he'd long since forgotten to hope for. As Kevin read the words to me, his voice husky with emotion, I realized for the first time ever that maybe someone could love me just for who I was. Who I was, it seemed, was finally enough.

Two weeks later, the night before I returned home to Mississippi, Kevin proposed marriage with another poem, and I said yes.

LATE SEPTEMBER 1976
MISSISSIPPI

My class elected me Senior Beauty this year, and today while we were having yearbook pictures taken, Kevin showed up. He had driven 750 miles, stopping only for gas. Motioning for me to come over to his car, he said we needed to leave. I said I couldn't do that, so he sat across the room watching me with angry eyes until the photographer had finished and then we left. Instead of driving me home, Kevin pulled into a remote old country cemetery, got out of the car, and lay down on one of the graves.

From where I was standing by the car, I asked, "What are you doing?"

"I think drugs have fried my brain," he responded and laughed.

"I thought you weren't taking drugs anymore," I replied.

"Oh, I'm not—this is old stuff."

Then he began saying how he felt God had given me a chance to either marry him or graduate from high school, but not both, and that I had to choose between worldly honors and pleasing God. When I reminded him that we were planning to be married *after* graduation, he simply replied that if I insisted on graduating, he could not marry me. Thinking, trying to decide what to do or say, I heard Kevin say, "Remember, you promised to marry me, so if you change your mind now, you'll be breaking your vow before God. And anyway—nobody else would have you."

Unfortunately, I couldn't argue with the logic of that.

Kevin got up off the grave, talking normally again, and took me home. Then he drove 750 miles back to his house, stopping only for gas.

Seven months later, a couple weeks before graduation, we were married, and within a matter of days, I began learning a new set of rules for behavior, an entire set of details to avoid and fear.

I cannot work as a search-and-rescue tracker without experiencing adrenaline levels that pause just this side of fear. But becoming overwhelmed by fear on a search—by the fear of failing, of missing a sign or being too late, of finding a dead body, perhaps a child's, of confronting the anger and grief of a family or the desperation of a suicidal person—succumbing to any of these apprehensions would mean I couldn't function well as a tracker. During the past nineteen years of my life I have become so closely acquainted with intense fear that managing low levels of it on a search is almost second nature.

For me, fear has become associated with small elements of the mundane—all the everyday things that I used to take for granted because there was no reason to do otherwise, things like laundry or tire tracks, folded handtowels or a door ajar, a footprint. But context is everything. Emotional context, for instance, mattered greatly. When Kevin was angry, laundry was often cause for a beating: if it was already done, he would throw it around the house, stomp through it, and then order me to clean it up; if it was being done, he would do the same; if it was undone, he simply beat me immediately and tossed the clothes nowhere because he hated unclean things and refused to touch them.

But physical context mattered too. At Kevin's house, for example, two perfectly folded handtowels meant that a beating possibly would be avoided, provided the space between them was exactly correct. So after leaving him, no matter where my children and I lived, we deliberately hung our towels sloppily—not out of postponed rebellion, but as a marker: If we ever came in and found two handtowels folded precisely in thirds and hung on the towel bar with exactly one inch of space between them, it meant that he had been in the house. And might still be there. That happened three times. Footprints where they should not have been were even more common—for eight years they showed up wherever we lived: in the soft grass outside our bedroom windows in the mountains, in the sandy dirt all around our house in the desert, and in the snow outside every place we ever lived where it snowed. Footprints still function as early warnings that someone has been around, urging caution and sometimes the need to leave quickly. They are still worth noticing.

So is a ringing telephone at two A.M. that goes dead when answered. Or a front door you locked leaving for work ten hours ago, now standing six inches ajar. These small details always have a history, in life and in tracking. There would be no reason to pay attention otherwise.

I am walking alone in a great, wide, flat basin—Forest Service land, I think, but really don't know, since I wasn't paying attention when we left the main highway. It has been three hours now that I have been walking here, looking down at a set of truck tracks, trying to make sure at each dirt crossing that I don't lose them. It's our second family vacation, and my husband Kevin, whom I married three years and two months ago today, brought me here in that truck, promising we wouldn't have any trouble this trip. But then this morning he drove us out here and said he'd only brought me along to get rid of me once and for all and that he was going to take Jon and find him a *good* mother somewhere. No one would ever even ask about me since I was "such a weirdo anyway," he said, holding his revolver pointed at my head while Jon slept soundly in his baby seat in the truck.

Laughing, Kevin cocked his gun and pointed it straight at me. When the cold steel touched my forehead, I shivered, and he laughed harder and said only the feeling of death running down my spine would cause me to shiver. Perhaps if I would apologize to him, he added, taking the gun away and pointing it toward a bird flying overhead, perhaps then he would consider sparing my life. I had no words at all, I could not think what I had done wrong. Kevin shot at the bird and missed, but the noise woke Jon from his nap and he called to me, "Mommy?" which broke through the terror that was holding me mute.

"I need to go to Jon—he's afraid," I said, and started to walk toward the truck when Kevin fired the gun at the ground next to my feet. Dust kicked up and then fell slowly back down. Kevin said, "If you move again, I'll put a bullet in that kid's brains before you take your second step." Walking quickly, he got into the truck, saying again that he would find Jon a good mother and that I'd never get out of this wilderness alive anyway—and then he drove away very fast, with Jon crying for me and me at first running after them, but then slowing to a walk as they disappeared.

I do not know why I continued to walk that day, following those tracks. All I knew was that one of my babies was in that truck, and I had to try to get to him. So I walked through that hot, almost treeless place—"as close to desert as a person could get without sand dunes," Kevin had said that morning.

Many times Kevin had remarked that if he ever really needed to get rid of a human body, the desert would be the place he would take it. He would say, "There nobody cares enough to ask questions about a leg that turns up in one county, or a head that shows up two counties over a couple months later," and then turn to me with a big smile, asking what I thought about him leaving my head in one county and a leg in another. I could never answer, such talk made me sick inside, quiet outside. Treeless places seemed not far from hell.

A few minutes before dark that evening the truck came back down the dirt track and stopped about thirty feet in front of me. Kevin yelled, "Hurry up and get in here," and before I could climb in, Jon was smiling and opening his arms wide for a hug.

For the next two days Kevin was almost happy: he even bought me a rose at a roadside stand just before we got home and said that maybe I wasn't as homely as it had seemed to him before. Roses make me queasy, but I smiled anyway: I was so happy to see real trees again.

From the poetry and philosophical discussions of early courtship to threats and blows a few months later. How could one man change so much? One week after our wedding, I saw the other side of Kevin's designer clothes: jeans had to be hung with an exact thumb's width (his thumb, not mine) between the hangers; clothes had to be sorted by color shades. Failure to meet these standards resulted in Kevin's throwing all the clothes in the closet onto the floor and ordering me to redo them. Within a month I had learned not to express any difference of opinion on any subject. But even if I stayed completely silent, my new husband always assumed I really disagreed with him "somewhere deep inside" and was as angry as if I had actually argued with him. Kevin's once-friendly smile too often became mocking and cruel. And even his poetry had changed: no longer about a young woman, hope, or love, it had turned inward and sinister and was commonly about things like "How to kill someone" or "A deal with Satan." The poems of courtship lost their beauty when Kevin told me they actually were written for another woman to whom he'd been engaged two years earlier—and still loved. But his voice, as he spoke of her, was so pained, his expression so wounded, that I felt only his grief and didn't realize that I could also have felt pain at having been deceived. Hope doesn't die easily when bolstered daily by strong, determined love.

It's been sixteen years since I walked along hating deserts and trying to follow the truck my son was in; fifteen years and eight months since my daughter was born; thirteen years since Kevin's and my divorce; and since that day deserts have become my most sacred places on earth. But let my eyes land on a set of tire tracks on a dirt road? I still get sick inside, quiet outside over things that can't be changed or even understood. Jon, Ruthie, and I have learned to walk on anyway, putting one foot in front of the other for as long as it takes, counting on things working out all right for all of us very soon. It's a tracker's brand of hope—which often turns out to be an effective tactic when you need to carry on in the face of fairly bad odds.

WALKING THROUGH FEAR

MUCH OF THE WORK trackers do is solitary: I could not begin to count the hundreds of hours I have spent alone outdoors, far from other humans. You become your own closest companion, the one person you have to be able to trust implicitly in any situation that might arise. Residual fears, the quirky ones we all carry around with us, a fear of heights or snakes, are fine associates for a tracker. But paralyzing ones, the kind that unhinge our abilities to trust ourselves or to think and observe clearly, are a serious detriment to a working tracker. You simply cannot follow someone else's footprints if you are scared witless.

As usual, though, life never gives us a neatly categorized set of anything, and fears are no exception. For me, the residual fears of childhood metamorphosed into the paralyzing terrors of early adulthood which meant that, in order to begin tracking at all (or even living fully), I had to confront them all together. And long before I'd ever considered becoming a tracker, that confrontation began.

AUGUST 1987
JOSHUA TREE NATIONAL MONUMENT

Hunched inside my poncho, temporarily outwitting the Mojave downpour, I sit on dry sand watching the edges of a footprint fold in on themselves when faced with the insistent, unexpected rainwater. In the desert everything bends to water's will: plants, animals, people, rocks, mountains, and tracks. Rainwater, perhaps even more than other water forms, dictates the terms of basic existence here. Insects, happily puttering along on a wash bottom, suddenly find themselves riding the crest of a muddy three-foot wave, bronco-busting the leading edge of a roiling flashflood. Desiccated ocotillo limbs shudder under the force of a summer thunderstorm and, hours later, launch green leaves from every socket and fiery red flags on top. Tiny grass seeds soak up as much of the floodwaters as they can and then propel blades upward to cover the desert floor for a few days with a delicate green blanket. Every living thing seems bent on expending its whole life's energy in those few precious moments after rain comes to the arid lands.

People, too, respond actively to water in the desert. Once, at the end of an eight-hour day in the hot summer sun, when a cloudburst unleashed itself upon my lonely head, I shed my pack, my clothes, and my inhibitions, and danced barefoot in fresh mud until daylight was gone, taking with it the double rainbow that had silently stood guard over the temporarily crazed mortal below. Then I put the bleeding soles of my feet back into their hiking boots and went home, as happy as if I had good sense.

Another young man wasn't so lucky. Inspired (or dared?) by deep water rushing through a canyon that had been dry five minutes earlier, he dove in to swim across. Hours later, a night with no moon shrouded the searchers who brought him out in a body bag. That was one search where there was no need for a tracker.

Tracks. They bring me back into this dry land, day after day. Like now, sitting on my heels, watching that one footprint in front of me. Mentally measuring the intensity of the storm, imprinting on my mind's eye the progression of changes in the track, watching it disintegrate and resist, cross-checking what I'm seeing with all the track conditions already filed in my brain, taking the time to memorize details (for time is one luxury trackers never have on a real search).

When it started to sprinkle today, time seemed to merge itself with the aridity lapsing momentarily beneath the storm, and both tiptoed off somewhere on the horizon to wait this one out. At the first raindrop on my cheek, I dropped my pack and stood still, face up, arms wide in a futile attempt to embrace all the raindrops before they hit the ground. Some days that's almost possible here—like on the afternoons when maybe ten raindrops per cloud fall, and any reasonably agile person can directly experience each one before the solitary cloud dissipates entirely. On other days the ground temperature is so high that raindrops vanish before they ever get within striking distance. Today the rain made me forget for a few minutes that I came out here to practice tracking, not meditation. But as the sky delivered its gentle droplets onto my celebrating head, I glanced over at the footprint and remembered my purpose.

For the first few minutes, the track I had been following held up nicely, allowing only a few audacious raindrops to decorate its surface with polka-dot patterns. As the sky darkened and emptied gallons of water (as opposed to the elfin teaspoons of moments before), both the footprints and I yielded. I, quickly, with a headlong dive toward my pack and rain poncho. The track was much more obstinate. Slowly its edges gave way to tiny rivulets of water, turning the polka dots into solids and the footprint into a memory.

Now, as the downpour subsides and the water hurries away from the desert again, the outlines of the track are slowly re-emerging. A little worse for wear, with rather rounded edges and its Adidas brand name no longer visible, but still maintaining its distinctive shape. I could follow this print with confidence anywhere, I think, glad as always for the rain. This time it taught me more about aging tracks in changing weather conditions.

Two hours later—after ninety minutes of a warm, drying wind—the footprint remained visible, even from thirty feet away. The wind dried me too, enough that the poncho could return to my pack, but still I sat, changing position periodically, watching the track, and making mental notes of the subtle color shifts it went through while drying out (rather like a cotton shirt on a clothesline). I watched two beetles and one cactus wren lay their own tracks across its surface, while tiny leaf pieces drifted in and were trapped by the ridge of sand around the track's heel.

Detritus—blowing bits of organic litter—is a fairly innocuous part of the desert's ecology. But what would happen to the world we know if traveling leaves decided to change the rules? To defy the certainty of sand wall traps around heel marks in the desert—to scale them and never come to rest anywhere?

Taking the litter out of the desert would be disastrous, ecologists tell us, and today a beetle confirms their findings. With the determination of a well-trained soldier, she climbs down into that heel print, chomps onto a leaf section much bigger than she is, and pulls it over the sand wall and into a hole several yards away. After she disappears, I glance back at the footprint, which now has a clear drag mark over the edge where the leaf has been hauled. The cactus wren was more interested in a small twig outside the track, but when she stopped to pick it up, she left her own footprint squarely in the middle, where "Adidas" had been before the rainstorm. Scientific questions reduced to their lowest common denominators: without detritus, what would beetles and birds do for home furnishings?

Sitting and thinking and watching. That's an important part of tracking. Patient attention to tiny, seemingly inconsequential details and differences. Measuring changes, memorizing patterns, asking intuitive questions and looking for their answers, ignoring sand in your eyes or rain on your head but imprinting on your mind the qualities of rain and sand located anywhere else.

Finding your own fears and blind spots, giving yourself a chance to measure their proportions, and then setting them aside so you'll have more time to sit and think and watch. And track.

Only two childhood fears—of snakes and heights—managed to stay with me into adulthood. All the rest were either educated or comforted away by my parents, grandparents, time and observation, or simple curiosity. After my father sang to me during a dry electrical storm one afternoon, I was no longer afraid of lightning. And when he and I stood in the bottom pasture as the eye of a hurricane passed over and felt its uncanny stillness before the winds returned, I figured hurricanes surely could not be too threatening if they had such calm hearts. Once my mother convinced me that living right meant I wouldn't go to hell, I no longer feared dying. Mammaw Ruth helped me learn that swift river currents were navigable, ponds were more dirty than dangerous, fishing worms can't bite people, and green lizards make some folks laugh and some run. Curiosity—or rather, a strong desire—to see a tornado alleviated any fear of them, especially after I finally saw and lived through one. I was always slightly afraid of the dark, of not being able to see clearly what was around me, but only my horror of heights and snakes remained fully entrenched—encouraged in no small part by my mother's example.

For a woman who has consistently been strong and fearless in most situations, my mother is surprisingly terrified of snakes or anything that remotely resembles one. Her fear is one of our family's grounding legends, eliciting fond if hearty laughter, usually prompted by my father, who is not the least bit afraid of snakes and likes to tease his wife and daughters about their "nonsense." His choice of noun is apt. Once Mama broke her wrist by running backward down a road from a snake that was trying to get away from her, and many times our farmwork was interrupted by the appearance of one of the dreaded reptiles—

and the resulting reverberations of tools and humans careening wildly about the place. But although the "nonsense" was highly entertaining later in stories, it was always completely rational to my sister Cassie and me during any snake event, so if we ever looked up to see Mama running, yelling, and waving her arms madly about, we ran and yelled too—instinctively. My mother's fear of heights was considerably quieter, expressed only on vacations in the Smoky Mountains, when she would insist on not sitting in the seat nearest the drop-off edge of the road, even if it meant Daddy had to pull over and she had to drive for a few miles. I dealt with that fear by crouching down on the floor of the truck or camper, knuckles clenched against eyelids, and praying for all I was worth until we reached flat ground again.

But these fears of childhood were fairly benign, and neither one caused serious harm until I married Kevin, shortly after celebrating my seventeenth birthday. For the next seven years, both fears worsened immeasurably. When someone sets out to control another person, to make her feel terror at whim, invoking childhood fears is an effective weapon. Kevin used both snakes and heights to full advantage—by the time I left him, just hearing the word "snake" would cause me to shake uncontrollably. My youthful fear of darkness was a different matter entirely. Kevin was afraid of the dark, you see, so it became almost safe for me: What he couldn't see, he couldn't hit, or even follow. During the first year of our marriage, before Jon was born, I ran from Kevin many times—into dark woods or along roadsides and railroad tracks—knowing that the darkness alone would shelter me for a time. With a child to consider, I could no longer run, nor could the dark grant safety. I was present in my own life with different feet.

Having a child made my reactions to Kevin's behavior even more crucial. Over and over Kevin said to me, "I'll make you mean if it's the last thing I do." Replying was both impossible and patently stupid, so I never tried. Nor did I ever attempt to hit back—with either words or actions. But though I was quiet outside, I always vowed fiercely to myself that at this one thing he would never succeed. "I'd rather be dead than mean" became my inner litany when Kevin would punch me and dare me to hit back "just once, if you have the guts." Hurting another person seemed tantamount to selling my soul. What kind of woman would my child have as a mother then? I clung to the litany and the questions no matter what Kevin did or said.

As things worsened and my death regularly seemed both imminent and inevitable, I grew more and more afraid that somehow I would change, become someone willing to hurt to escape my own pain. Death itself was not at all frightening. To become cruel to others, oblivious to or even reveling in their pain as Kevin did—this was (and is) my greatest nightmare, the one fear I cannot shake, that I feel I must guard against always.

Tracks. What is it about them that could have forced me to excise part of my previous self? Paralyzed by my fear of snakes by the time I was twenty-seven, I could well have lived to be an old woman harboring the terrors of childhood and a cruel marriage. My mother, at least, would've understood the grip of the old fears. But what she doesn't fathom to this day—and what I've only recently begun to appreciate—is that those old patterns began to fall apart when I started trying to follow footprints in desert sand.

Fear cannot dog a tracker's every move, for if it does, she soon tires, losing the edge that is necessary to keep the eyes and mind alert no matter how long they have been working. Beyond that, fear tugs at intuition until the tracker's ability to think beyond herself gets hopelessly entangled in doubts and emotional flailings. Fear, however useful in other circumstances, ruins a tracker's day, for it makes the tracks hard to see and even harder to follow.

Following. An odd concept at best, given the lone natures of many trackers. I was first drawn to this work by its antisocial qualities—the many hours of tramping about alone in the backcountry, the precise observations and vivid experiences that are required, the demands for intense physical and mental exertion, none of which need another human's immediate presence. Working alone, I sought to immerse myself in the desert's rhythms.

The desert doesn't heal the pain of losing one's children or even numb it, but rather layers and pigeonholes it for you so that grief doesn't overwhelm, cries don't deafen, and tears don't postpone anything. In the desert your terror passes for courage, reassuring everyone but yourself, and somehow in the midst of all that certainty, you realize that you are surviving. As a tracker, I was not only surviving, but following the footprints of other human beings, well on the way to becoming human again myself. Going to the desert to escape people, I quickly began searching for them again in the most literal way imaginable: following their tracks. Always hoping that one day the tracks I followed would lead me to my own children, back home with me, safe and unharmed and happy at last. In the interim, tracking had to keep me sane, had to keep the grief from becoming self-destruction, had to fuel the search for those paths back to other people, those connections to a life that had gone so hopelessly awry. Given those charges, I had no choice but to track—which meant that I had to walk through my fears.

⸻

"One way to get over being afraid of snakes," Frank announced one afternoon as he brought in a small rosy boa, "is to live with one for a while—watch him move, touch him, find out he's not slimy or dangerous."

Unconvinced, I watched from the other side of the room as Frank gently settled the small greyish reptile into a sandy-bottomed terrarium next to the stereo. With my usually rational husband promising on Scout's Honor (which I don't entirely trust anyway—having seen a few too many Boy Scouts rampaging through national parks) that the holes in the lid were too small for the snake to fit through, I reluctantly agreed to watch this new resident for a few days.

"But touching is out of the question," I grumbled, making a mental note to check that the lid was securely on every hour, day or night.

Lid-checking quickly became a series of extended "visits" to the terrarium: by the second one, I was sitting on the floor a couple feet away, watching this small, sinuous creature explore his new home. By the fourth, I had to wait cross-legged on that hard floor for more than an hour because Bo (named sometime during the third "visit") was curled up into a tight, unmoving ball in the dark corner of his terrarium. When he finally unkinked himself and groggily moved into the sunshine, I was sitting on my knees in front of the terrarium, elbows propped up on the shelf underneath the snake's home, nose (and eyes) only inches away from the glass.

"So—want to hold him a while?" Frank's unexpected return

startled me into an excellent imitation of my mother: arms flying wildly, I jumped up and back, sending cassette tapes and a glass of ice water flying (but not once actually touching that terrarium). As Frank laughed and mopped up ice cubes and water, I dried off cassette tapes and finally recovered enough to point out that the snake was probably really hungry by now. By the time we had finished mopping ice water off our living room floor, Frank had completed my first mini–natural history lesson (snakes won't eat lettuce, raisins, nuts, seeds, or anything else easily obtained—they like eggs and birds and mice, preferably live ones). Frank's plan for Bo's meals solved two problems at once. Deer mice had been raiding my vegetables every night for a month, the snake needed food, and my garden had an overabundance of his favorite victuals, so a live trap was clearly the only moral option.

Ten minutes later, when the trap door swung shut on the first mouse, I wasn't feeling so unequivocally moral or anti-mouse. Deer mice are really quite cute little creatures, with their wide brown eyes and tiny feet, so I hurried inside with the trap—only to look into those eyes and rush right back out again, justifying the absurdity of freeing the mouse by saying that "This one is too big—Bo would choke." After three tries, we finally caught a small mouse and I steadfastly refused to look into its eyes (focusing instead on the pile of seedlings that it and its relatives had mown down that very morning) while Frank dropped it into Bo's sandy house. After a couple of nervous quick-steps, the mouse hunkered down and sat perfectly still, while I sat watching, arguing first for letting the mouse go back and eat up the whole garden if it wished and then for getting some food into Bo (who was looking quite emaciated).

Apparently unbothered by similar ethical dilemmas, Bo immediately began hunting. Slowly he inched himself into position as the mouse sat still, wary, but not yet aware that it was being stalked. Suddenly Bo struck—and the mouse leapt away, reflexively attuned to the danger. Gone was the waiting pose. Now the mouse was watching, listening, no doubt measuring the size, the skill, the determination of its adversary. Running up onto a slanting dead branch, it sat still at the top, and as Bo slowly slid underneath (some six inches below), the mouse jumped off the branch—right onto Bo's head—and then ran around the terrarium and back to the top of the branch. Off onto Bo's head it catapulted itself again, this time jumping up and down several times before climbing the branch and repeating the process. On the second pass, the mouse actually bit at Bo, who tried in vain to reorient himself enough to strike back.

By the third attack I was frantic and Bo was looking decidedly dazed, so I yanked that mouse out between jumps and returned it to the garden with a little more force than was entirely civilized or necessary. After two more tries, with even smaller deer mice, one thing seemed crystal clear: deer mice are born with genetic instructions for killing snakes—jump up and down on their heads repeatedly and then chew them in two at any convenient point on their bodies. It seemed to me that the mice had every intention of eating Bo for dinner, rather than being eaten by him.

So, early the next morning, I headed for the nearest pet store that sold pinkie mice (newborns). The first trip back home, through sixty miles of 115 degree heat, they all died in my car (which had no air conditioner), and Bo wouldn't even consider eating them. In fact, for all the interest he showed, I might as well have offered him a bundle of rocks for dinner. On the second trip,

I put the pinkies inside an ice chest; they froze and Bo refused again, no more interested in frozen than he had been in baked mouse. For the third trip in as many days, I made an elaborate insulated container out of Goretex ski leggings, wool socks, and newspapers; this time the pinkies survived both the ice chest and the outside air, and Bo had his first good meal since coming to live at our house.

Clearly, by this point—willingly sacrificing tiny, newborn mice to a snake—I had begun replacing an irrational fear with fairly irrational behavior. But pinkie mice have no open eyes with which to challenge a conscience. After only a couple feedings, though, none of what I was doing felt ethical: soon afterward I was moving rattlesnakes off sidewalks, roads, and out of campsites as if herpetology was my first love, and Bo was fending for himself against the deer mouse population of the southern California desert. I'd be willing to bet he probably never travels under branches of any kind. And I still stay out of the mouse section of all pet shops.

But I also still get out of my car—no matter where I am—and move sunbathing snakes off roads so that the next vehicle won't hit them. And, according to my mother at least, *that* is fairly irrational behavior. Nor does she believe me when I tell her that snakes aren't slimy at all.

Dogged determination serves most folks well, but one of the best character traits a tracker can have is patience, large amounts of it, too. I was not born patient—my mother says I came two months early, cut my first tooth at three months, and have been hurtling pell-mell ever since—waiting was never my strong suit.

The years with Kevin meant that I had to learn patience: Waiting, in fact, was preferable most times to what followed it. But tracking? Now there's where I learned not just to *be* patient, but to like it.

I've been lying on my stomach here in the middle of Fried Liver Wash since noon; Sam, my search dog puppy, is stretched out in the shade behind me. Tranquil doesn't begin to describe this place. The air is still, not even a whisper in the dry creosote branches, and the sky lies well back on the horizon. Without provocation, a dry lupine stalk drops one of its leaves, and a lizard's tail barely misses it as he scurries across the hot sand, heading for the next shady spot. There's a sidewinder coiled up under a smoke tree a few yards away—she and I have been eyeing each other warily ever since I stumbled across her track, startling her into a defensive posture. When I sat down in the middle of the wash, she watched a few seconds and then quickly moved closer to the base of the tree, carefully adjusting her body backward in short undulating sweeps. Very graceful. Funny how I never noticed that rattlesnakes were graceful before today. My mother would undoubtedly disagree.

When I switched positions, lying down and adjusting my hat to avoid the sun, the sidewinder arched and looked my way crossly, settling down into a full coil. Since then, we have both been sitting here mostly motionless. I brushed a fly off my face a couple times and she rearranged her coils once, but other than that, we've been still as dead mice. I intend to stay until she moves again, so that I can see exactly how she makes those odd J-shaped tracks. Sam, content to stay if I am, is sound asleep.

Far overhead, a buzzard rides what appears to be a decent headwind and circles down closer to see who's newly dead in the wash. I wave to him so he realizes we're not dinner fixings yet, and he goodnaturedly wends his way toward the Eagle Mountains. Four Huey helicopters putter their way north toward the Marine Corps Base, and a cactus wren from somewhere nearby shouts her annoyance at the disturbance. Actually, she was shouting before the Hueys came by, so any annoyance is probably all mine. Sam looks up, yawns, rolls onto his back, and falls asleep again. Even the sidewinder looks relaxed now, and as the sounds of the Hueys fade, mindful of the desert's hints, the tension in my neck also begins to subside. Annoyance with the military is useless anyway; in southern California it's like tilting at windmills, only less productive.

The sidewinder, after one last glance in my direction, finally decides to continue with her day by heading up the slight incline behind the smoke tree. With quick, deft movements, she slips sideways up the hot sand, etching her eccentric trail. Sand grains slowly slide down to rest in the lowest part of each track as she moves along, body touching the hot ground at two points only and undulating back and forth in between them. Considering how long I've been waiting here to watch this very thing happen, you'd think I would be able to describe it better. But there are no words precise enough to convey the snake's delicate balance, her swift and steady movements, or the certainty with which she's heading up that hill. Clearly she knows where she is going. Sam and I just watch.

Since I don't know where we're going—or, more accurately, since we don't have anywhere to go this afternoon—I continue to sit in the wash and watch the snake's tracks change as the sun begins to drop lower in the sky. Sam takes another nap. The longer the shadows get, the more visible the tracks are. That's why tracking at high noon is so difficult—without shadows to throw them into relief, tracks might as well not be there. Trackers have to adjust to the flat light conditions of midday: We sometimes use mirrors to backlight the tracks, after shading them with our caps—a slow, painstaking process that is hard on both eyes and patience.

Tracks in sand, like those the sidewinder just left, are relatively easy for the tracker to see no matter what the light conditions, but tracks on scrub rocks practically disappear in flat light. Even shaded and backlit, they're elusive at best, so sometimes the wisest strategy for noon tracking is simply to sit down and eat lunch. Since a nap afterward is a luxury Sam and I wouldn't have on an actual search, in practice sessions we make the most of the opportunity. Today I roll over into the shade next to my dog and we both doze off, soothed by the heat that surrounds us like a warm oven.

Two hours later. The sidewinder has been gone a long time now, and the sun is leaving the sky, washing it with the brilliant hues of a smog-induced sunset. Bats are already out, fluttering and zinging their way up and down the wash, searching for the insects they live on and we think we could live without. A cool evening breeze slightly lifts the branches of a creosote bush and softly rattles through a dry desert trumpet stem. Nearby the birdcage skeleton of one of last year's evening primroses sits placidly as the wind sends tiny particles of sand and plant matter sweeping though its open railings. Somewhere off to the east a coyote yips and another answers from the mountains, and then another and another and another, until the night is ringed with coyote song. Ears full, eyes tired, Samson and I walk down the wash toward the car.

Bounding a few feet ahead, Sam sniffs around under a creosote bush, but the instant I yell, "Samson, *leave!*" he whips around and waits for my next words. His immediate obedience may have just saved his nose: At the base of the bush another sidewinder sits coiled, ready to strike at this offensive blond intruder. Sam gallops happily back to me, entirely unaware of the danger behind him, so I snap on his leash, put him on heel and walk up to the bush. Pointing at the snake, I repeat, "Leave." Sam's face first registers the snake, then the command. Not two seconds later, he is ready to continue down the wash, as uninterested in the motionless snake as if it were a rock. I make him stay to watch the snake leave so he will associate the coiled creature with the moving one, repeating the command "Leave" each time he starts to step toward the sliding, retreating reptile. Suddenly Sam looks up, and I can see that he's figured it out. He now knows snakes are off-limits—he can be counted on to avoid them by himself next time. He will tell me with his eyes that one of those strange things is nearby—as any good search partner would—but he won't go bounding into it and wind up getting bitten. The first snake was my teacher, the second one his. We have learned good lessons today, he and I, sitting in the hot sun and walking home at dusk.

For several months I watched snakes in the desert in all kinds of weather, for hours on end, seeing how they moved and never once finding one that seemed remotely aggressive. Finally I learned to pick them up and move them off the road or out of campsites, to identify their favored spots, and to enjoy sharing the arid land with them. In the process, one childhood fear disappeared and left some odd residues—cheerful patience, for one. Others underwent more subtle transformations.

Heights—of whatever magnitude—became my nemesis in third grade, when I fell out of a tree I wasn't supposed to be climbing in the first place and hurt important parts of my body. As a child I didn't care to examine the fear, and I certainly never considered overcoming it. High places scared me—it was really that simple—so I stayed very close to the ground.

Living in Mississippi made that rather easy to do. The gentle, rolling hills around our farm were so low that I had no concept of a lofty landscape for the first few years of my life. But that soon changed, thanks to an odd cultural notion my parents embraced when I turned eight: family vacations, two of them while I was growing up, and both to the same place, the Smoky Mountains. These trips for me were nightmares of narrow, winding roads with shoulders that dropped abruptly into thin air. My sister Cassie, four years younger, loved the mountains. I did too, at least the trees and ferns and bears and squirrels and deer that lived there, but I would have enjoyed all those things far more had they been located on flat ground.

Years later, several months after moving to Jackson, Wyoming, I realized one day that the Teton mountains made the Smokies look like southern speedbumps. But the Jackson Hole valley was flat and I was numb, so I forgot all about the mountains for a few months, especially during the time that our survival seemed least likely. After seven years of marriage, the last month of which had convinced me that it was only a matter of time until Kevin killed Jon, Ruthie, and me, I had taken my children and left their father. Leaving was not some desperate attempt to survive—far from it, for I had no doubt whatsoever that Kevin would eventually find us and that he would then finish what he had started: survival was not a possibility I knew how to conceptualize then.

The man I had married had become a maniacal pseudo-stranger, vaguely familiar but now continually crazed, someone who regularly beat or choked me unconscious and watched me constantly. Every meal I cooked during the last month ended with his sweeping dishes and food off the table and pounding my head and body against the kitchen wall, taunting, screaming that if I would just fight back once he would stop. I could neither eat nor sleep because at least once a day, every day of that month, Kevin told me that he intended to make me watch him torture and kill Jon and Ruthie before dismembering me and leaving my body parts scattered through the desert. There was no "reason" for the violence anymore—no attempt to blame me because I had burned the corn while cooking dinner, forgotten the butter knife when setting the table, placed too many ice cubes in his glass, or left only a three-quarter-inch space between the two handtowels on the bathroom towel bar. Kevin by then had plenty of money, was self-employed, and lived an upper-middle-class life, complete with a skinny, passive, obedient wife and two bright, beautiful children, new houses and vehicles and designer clothing. None of the violence made sense.

One evening Kevin beat me for several hours, a cycle which had become utterly routine. Stopping intermittently to sit in a chair, clicking a switchblade open and shut in his hand, watching me lie bleeding on the floor across the room, he would then begin to yell and come toward me once more. Finally he hauled Jon and several guns into the bedroom, vowing to kill my son if he heard any sound at all. I spent that night crouching in a corner at the farthest end of the house, holding my daughter in my arms and quieting her, my hand over her mouth, when she awoke whimpering. The next evening, Kevin beat me again and choked me unconscious. My last thought before blacking out was that this time I would die — leaving my children alone with this man. Kevin then dragged me into the bedroom, put me on the bed, and forced me to lie there beside him all night. Too numb to feel fear, something finally snapped. Unable to see or speak, I lay listening to Kevin ranting about people coming to get him, his screams so intense that they shook the whole bed, and decided that if I lived through the night, I would take Jon and Ruthie and run away. At least I would not die cowering in a corner. Less than thirty hours later, five minutes after Kevin had left the house on a brief errand, I fled. Kevin hired someone to track us down: he found us in Wyoming three weeks later, and the terror continued unabated for the next two years, with Kevin periodically surfacing, threatening to kill us all.

Wyoming in no way became home because of the beauty of its rugged scenery, but because there—for the first time—we found a whole community of people who were staunchly opposed to domestic violence. The grandeur of the mountains did not speak to my frozen emotions; they stood as monumental witnesses to the various thugs who would show up to "knock some sense" into me, threatening to kidnap the three of us and take us back to Kevin (where we "belonged"), or simply to sit across the road in plain view to terrorize us with the certainty that they could come in whenever they decided to do so.

In the shadow of those silent mountains I faithfully put on every single day the bulletproof vest given to me by a police lieutenant; a bedraggled copy of a restraining order sat between a

.357 revolver and the container of mace in my purse; and an ever-growing stack of legal papers filled my closet, chronicles of my attempts to convince an Oklahoma court that no man should have the right to beat us. Yet before each day had ended I had questioned at least once whether it might not be better to just take off the vest, throw the gun and mace away, and die quietly?

But the trusting eyes of a three-year-old daughter and five-year-old son always stiffened my fading resolve to face violence with violence if I had to. The gun and vest were continual reminders of the central paradox in my life: though I had vowed never to become "mean," I wore a bulletproof vest so that I might survive a first shot—and carried a gun so that I could have some chance of saving my children's and my lives. Kevin's threats became almost routine, and my children and I were well known at the battered women's shelter.

Then one day—a day lost in darkness for me—Kevin disappeared with Jon and Ruthie. The next morning, he called and, with Ruthie screaming "Mommy, Mommy!" in the background, said, "Now you've lost them for good, bitch and—SHUT UP, you damn brat!"—I went into a deep dark place of grief. Weeks later I finally resurfaced—and turned to the mountains.

Why? That's hard to say. Somehow only the mountains could encompass the terror that consumed me, now that Jon and Ruthie had no one to protect them from the man who had beaten me for seven years. Only the mountains could contain my screams and my furious helplessness—no money, no chance of finding my children, no hope of ever seeing them alive again. Sick and frightened and exhausted, I could hear only Ruth's screams and Jon's silence echoing again and again through a chilling reality: The U.S. legal system does not work for people who have no money. And according to the judge in our own case anyway, while it was legal for a man to beat his wife and children, it was illegal for a woman to desert her husband. I had deserted Kevin—and now to fight for the return of my children would require more money than I could ever hope to find.

Dry-eyed, I took to wandering through the foothills, aimlessly walking myself into a stupor so that I could find sleep, however fitful. While other people carried bird books and marveled at the life around them, I walked alone, avoided everybody, carried and noticed nothing, not even the eagles or highest peaks. Head most often down, not the least bit interested in seeing the mountains or anything on them, I simply walked the spring months away. Across scree slopes so unstable I'd slide down two feet with every forward step. Up grades so steep that losing my grip on a root or branch meant I'd tumble head over heels back to the bottom. Through deep snow to the treeline. Back down to the valley's muddy floor and into the temporary creeks of the season's thaw.

But one summer day something again snapped inside—suddenly I realized that if I could survive, Jon and Ruthie could too. Sharply alive again, for the first time in months, I touched the rock I was sitting on, wondering how long it and I had been there. Starting down, it became clear that in my right mind I wouldn't have been caught dead up on that particular rock— which, I now noticed, ended in a vertical drop of about three hundred feet. My fear of heights came roaring back to life, pinning me to the rock, while the sun's rays grew longer. Finally I managed to inch my way to the next safe sitting spot, where I sat shaking until the cold night air began closing in. When it was no longer clear whether I was shivering from cold or fear, I decided it was time to get off that rock.

Scared but determined, I gingerly started out—only to collapse with laughter, genuine peals of it. How ironic it would be if, after the hell of the last seven years, I wound up dead from falling off a *rock*?! After a number of stops to control my giggles—and my shaking knees—I finally stepped off granite and onto dirt and sat down and cried right there, for the first time in years.

My yes, by then those mountains knew me much better than any human could have. People tend to run from tears and trouble; mountains just stand and watch, silently offering some of their ageless strength to the small lost souls who collapse at their feet. But mountains also just stand and mutely watch humans fall to their deaths fairly regularly too, so the next day I signed up for climbing school—one lesson, fifteen dollars, which was more than I could afford—and from then on climbed every chance I got. Meeting Frank, a park ranger in the Grand Tetons who became my friend and eventually my second husband, meant that I soon had a climbing mentor, which helped immensely. And although my fear of heights barely subsided for the first two years of climbing, I soon learned that swearing was an excellent way to keep my muscles from locking up when I was petrified. For one raised not to say even the word "darn," I rapidly developed a full vocabulary of the most shocking words, and halfway up every climb—which was always the crux for me—I'd run through my new vocabulary at least twice, make up a few new words for good measure, promise god that if she helped me get down safely I'd never get on a rock again, and then head for the top, where Frank would grin at me, make some irreverent comment about my language, and ask what climb I wanted to try next.

So, with Frank moderating his pace (and his desire for challenges), off we went from Wyoming's Tetons to Colorado's Flatirons, to West Virginia's Seneca Rocks and California's Yosemite Valley, with me scared on every climb and swearing the last half of it away. Then at last we moved to Joshua Tree National Monument in the southern California desert, where I finally had a good fall right near the end of a climb up a short, grungy little wall. Moments later, standing on the top, peering over the edge past my bleeding knee, trying to figure out why I'd lost my footing, annoyed that I hadn't taken my first fall on a "clean line" (an aesthetically pleasing route), it suddenly dawned on me that dying while climbing would not be a bad way to go. I have not been afraid of heights or cursed on a climb since.

For the tracker I was rapidly becoming, that moment was a watershed: climbing and tracking became tools, rather than crutches, and life too long to pine away. The fierce longing for Jon and Ruthie erupted in productive activity—if I couldn't have my own children, I would at least give something back to other people. I had started tracking almost accidentally, but the realization that tracking could save the life of somebody's child offered me a chance to rejoin the world and sent me into the desert every day for months.

Having survived repeated beatings by the man I'd vowed—and then done my damnedest—to love "for better or worse" had me convinced that there was no savior anywhere, least of all in the wild places we designate as "nature." When you are being hunted down, deer trails are merely countrified versions of city streets; they lack streetlights and traffic and crowds, and that makes them marginally safer. When you are tormented, mountains are obstacle courses for the mind and body—noticing their beauty only leaves you more vulnerable to your own pain. Nothing at all in nature can save us from society.

When there's no savior, faith doesn't enter into the equation. In the final decision to leave, you get out blindly, dumbly, knowing that when (not if) he catches up with you, he's going to kill you and your children. So why even leave? Because somewhere deep inside, something shattered that last time he choked you—from a place long forgotten, you finally decided that if you had to die, you at least would not do so cowering in a corner of his house. So yes, I left. Took those two little children by the hand and walked. Put one foot in front of the other. For a very long time indeed.

Tracking isn't instinctive or natural. It only begins when you start seeing the ground under your feet instead of just staring blindly at it; when you acknowledge the pain, accept the uncertainty of hope, feel the fear of being saviorless, yet insist not simply on surviving but also on paying attention to the small details of life once again. Tracking means immersing yourself in signs and in the knowledge that none of us goes anywhere without leaving a trail behind—a pretty damned reassuring thought when you're being stalked by someone who has sworn to kill you, laughing because "no one will care enough to even inquire about where you've gone."

Tracking also means learning to walk alongside, caring enough to reach out to other people—a crucial part of surviving when someone wants to make sure you don't. To me, perhaps most of all, tracking in 1986—newly married to Frank, living in Joshua Tree, having somehow survived eighteen months without my children—meant making a commitment to life. It meant facing memories and fears head-on, no more cringing in submission. Above all else, tracking meant patience: at a time when waiting was often the only thing I could do to bring my children home to me, it meant sitting quietly and watching my own existence, trying to understand the significance of the J-shaped tracks each of us leaves behind as we move through life. Learning, in short, to walk alongside myself.

LOSING THE WAY

THE PROCESS of getting lost seems complex and lengthy on the surface, but it quite often is nothing of the sort. Two steps off the trail for whatever reason—flower gazing, birdwatching, rock photography, or a simple nap—and you can be just as lost as if somebody had dumped you fifty miles from the nearest building. There's no rationale behind losing your way, but trackers have to at least try to understand the process before attempting to find someone. Tracking one's life is much the same. Sometimes you have to figure out why you did a thing in order to know what it was that you actually did. Retracing steps requires getting alarmingly close to what is most unknown to us: who we were at a specific point in time. Who we were without ever knowing it.

———

What is it about the desert that brings out the irrational in some people? Is there something lurking in austere lines and immense distances that elicits human stupidity, that begs us to lose ourselves in a place we don't know? Why would anybody think that putting on a blindfold in the middle of the night and walking through the Mojave (standard practice in the desert survival courses held in Joshua Tree National Monument a few years ago) would enhance one's chances of surviving in the desert in a real crisis? Why would a troop leader outfit fifteen boys with knives and survival myths, then hit the trail only to walk off and leave one of those boys behind, somewhere along the way because "he was lagging"? Why would a Marine think he could walk through an unfamiliar sixteen square miles of rock boulders without a map, compass, guide, or canteen? Why would another man try to drive a Ford Mustang through the Monument—southbound in a dry wash—in hopes of reaching Palm Springs? Hubris, or worse, seems to affect a lot of people in the desert.

But not all accidents in the desert are the result of macho or even demonstrably irrational behavior. Some of them are simply the consequences of small mistakes in judgment, of only slightly offbeat wrong turns, the kind we humans sometimes make in spite of our best intentions. Why would a grown man decide to lie flat on his back to commune with the stars on a dark Mojave night in the middle of a deserted road? Why would a family decide that since Grandma is too tired to finish the hike, everyone else will continue while she walks back a quarter mile to the campsite to rest? Why would a young woman choose to take a desert hike wearing nothing but a bikini and sandals? Why would a climber decide to free-solo a route that she knows is at the limits of her best ability? How could someone raised to value humility above most human virtues wake up one morning to find that she has been behaving in a decidedly arrogant fashion?

For I, too, began to lose my way in the desert, but I was well on the path to becoming a professional search-and-rescue tracker working mostly for the National Park Service before I wakened enough to notice that I was lost. And, true to form, my first reaction was to run.

What would happen to humans if we could know the outcomes of our decisions in advance? Would we behave differently at the outset? Change our choices before they had a chance to change us? Maybe.

MARCH 1986
The first Sunday after Frank and I moved to Joshua Tree National Monument, I laced up my hiking boots and set off for the visitor center in search of enlightenment. One of our two neighbors, Tim, a seasonal Park Service naturalist, was leading a walk to Cottonwood Oasis. I intended to tag along. Within minutes we were off, a lively, interested group of mostly senior citizens, Tim, and me. Wearing his Smokey the Bear hat and carrying a green pack, Tim was young, witty, and diplomatic. As we walked, he rattled off so many Latin names and plant, animal, and bird characteristics that every last one of us was impressed, me probably most of all. I had always been in awe of Park Service employees, first in the Smoky Mountains as a child, then in the

Great Sand Dunes and Yellowstone and the Grand Tetons and Death Valley and every other park I'd visited as an adult, but this particular ranger put the rest to shame. He knew everything there was to know about the desert. And he was my next-door neighbor: This was going to be a fun place to live.

Cottonwood Oasis, even when you know it's there, is still a surprise. We were scrambling along through widely scattered boulders, walking parallel to the road but out of sight of it, when suddenly Cottonwood Canyon stretched out to the right. Directly down the ridge in front of us nestled a clump of palm trees, mesquite, and waterworn stones. From this vantage point above the canyon floor, Tim fairly sparkled with excitement, pointing out one bird after another. Trying to pay close attention, but knowing full well I wasn't seeing half of the identifying marks he was pointing out—for that matter, I wasn't even seeing all of the birds, much less their markings—I managed to stand still for a few minutes. But eventually I decided that the thing I really wanted to do was get down to that oasis. To stand under those palm fronds instead of above them, like a wounded duck staring mournfully up at the sky.

So that's where I headed, in the most tactful way possible. Years of ditching groups on school field trips had given me skills along this line. Already at the back of the group, I began edging my way to the left. Every time Tim pointed out another bird, I'd shade my eyes with my right arm and move left as if to see better where he was pointing. Two minutes later I took my last hypocritical look at some bird blur rising up into the sky—then scrambled down the hillside toward the upper end of the canyon, out of sight of Ranger Tim and the senior citizens. All but one of them, that is. A spry bald-headed man with a grin the size of Tim's hat brim had figured out what I was doing and decided to come along. "Never can see those damn birds," he said emphatically as he came alongside.

"Me neither."

We didn't say anything else (I have always liked people who are quiet when they're outdoors), but plunged into the brush above the spring, the source of the oasis' water. In a few minutes we were sitting on damp, water-polished rocks, listening to the trickle of water and watching it spill over the rock edges to the sand below where it quickly disappeared. Soon the group came down the pathway with Tim still pointing out winged things.

"That boy sure knows his birds, doesn't he?" the man said, shaking his head.

"His birds, his flowers, his trees, even his grasses—isn't it amazing how they can learn so *many* things about a place?" I replied, shaking my head too.

"Sure is—must go through years of schooling," the man nodded, and we crawled down the slippery rocks to rejoin the group.

On the way back to the visitor center, I dawdled along at the end of the line, not particularly eager to go home and continue unpacking. Tim waited for me and asked, "So how did you like your first guided tour of Cottonwood?"

"It was great!" I replied—and was just about to add an effusive compliment when one of the women ahead called out in a perplexed tone, "Ranger, can you tell me what this lovely little flower is?"

Tim was immediately back on the job. "Let me see," he said, walking briskly toward the spot where the woman was standing a few feet away. Without even bending down, he looked at the tiny bunch of flowers and said, "Oh, that's what's commonly known as desert calico—or eriophyllum. You'll find it all along here."

The group gathered around and oohed and aahed, then slowly started off again. I stayed crouched down looking at the flowers with the woman who'd asked the question. She kept saying to herself in a southern accent, "Calico—eriophyllum. Desert calico. Eriophyllum. Such a lovely little thing, isn't it?" then hurried off to rejoin the others. I just sat on my heels looking at the dark pink, almost purple blooms. Desert calico my foot.

Tim was waiting for me and the words were out of my mouth before I could think them back. "Hey Tim, that's purple mat. *Nama demissum.*"

"Oh really?" he said, continuing to walk.

"Yeah—it's one of the two I know. Why did you tell them it was desert calico?"

Tim shrugged absentmindedly and nodded toward the backs of the people ahead of us. "They'll never know the difference. So they want a name? I give it to them and we're all happy." He grinned and then added, disarmingly frank, "I know the birds and that's about it. The flowers and bushes all look alike to me, but I'm a park ranger so I have to answer their questions."

"Can't you just tell them you don't know?"

"Oh *sure*—and be out of a job next season? No thanks, whatever I think of first works just fine."

We chatted neighborly things on the way home, and Tim offered to come over one evening to show me a Bendire's thrasher, one of his favorite birds, which frequented my backyard every spring. Then I went home and avoided unpacking by looking up in four separate wildflower guides the desert calico, eriophyllum, and purple mat. They were three entirely different flowering plants, and the only eriophyllum I could find was yellow.

Wildflowers are addictive; their Latin names seductive. Once you learn one flower's proper, scientific name and feel compelled to search through five field guides for another one, you are in trouble. And once you spend thirty minutes on your knees in a sandy wash only to realize you haven't found the right species after all—yet you get up still searching—you are a goner. But on the day you decide that wildflower classifications are worth either faking (as Tim did) or insisting on (as I eventually did), you may well have been sucked into the vortex of Nature with a capital N. Thoroughly lost, for all intents and purposes.

Tracking requires no knowledge of the scientific names of plants. Nor does a tracker need to stay abreast of the latest academic squabbles over correct classification of any plant. Working as a naturalist—even only as a volunteer—in the National Park Service, though, demands more than a passing acquaintance with both. The demand is seldom stated outright, for like many cultural norms this one is communicated through more subtle means—the way a learned person raises her eyebrows slightly on hearing someone else misidentify a plant, for example.

Already-acculturated spouses and friends tend to be considerably less subtle. When every hike is interspersed with stops not just to look at or to photograph flowers, but to pull out several field guides to identify them, the unacculturated one should soon grasp the significance of the activity. If not, she will surely begin to do so when the flower is next sighted—and hailed by its Latin name, followed by a verbal ticking off of its key botanical features. And on the morning she refuses to leave her house without stuffing six or seven field guides (weighing several pounds) into her daypack, you can be sure that she has learned the lesson so well she's nearing the point of believing that being lost in Nature is a normal state of affairs. Soon she too will be raising an eyebrow when someone misidentifies a flower or mammal track, then gently correcting the mistake; rattling off Latin names even when they're utterly unnecessary; sounding confident, sure of an obscure taxonomy because she spent four hours last night studying it, passionately determined not ever to be a "fake."

Being lost in Nature but unwilling to feign knowledge is hard work: Every time I had to say "I don't know" to a tourist, I would spend whatever time was necessary that night learning the answer to the question. More times than I would have cared to admit back then, I wished for some of Tim's chutzpah, his ability to not know, to lie, and to keep walking without a backward glance. Tim's breezy approach to authority and knowledge was not an anomaly in the Park Service, and his joking reference to being out of a job if the holes in his knowledge were discovered had a serious undertone. People expect rangers (and other such experts) to have answers.

So while purple mat is a fine name for a wildflower, very descriptive and simple to remember, *Nama demissum* singles out the rememberer as one of a fairly elite group. Environmental elites remember things that other people forget; they recall them quickly, easily, confidently; they seldom if ever have to say, "I don't know the answer to that question"; and they can even go one better: they can tell you categorically how humans should behave in the rainforest or the Sahara, on a volcano's edge or mountain's treeline, in a city park or cornfield. The day I unconsciously set out to join that group, I was well on my way down a wrong path. But that's hindsight. Twenty-twenty or better every time.

Some of the experts who work for the National Park Service, and many environmentalists who simply visit the parks, are skilled in the art of identifying bad human habits in Nature, and they're even better at convincing the person with the habit that it needs changing—yesterday, preferably. This insight didn't come so much from observation as from experience: During the first few months I spent in National Park Service areas, I kept everybody busy breaking my bad habits. Not intentionally, to be sure, but regularly enough so that no one could have mistaken me for an environmentally correct specimen of the human species. Some would no doubt have thought "heathen" was a more appropriate label for me in those days.

After all, returning from a hike through a canyon with a daisy behind your ear is clear evidence of criminal genetic makeup, no? Even picking up a dead leaf is suspect behavior, so imagine the horror aroused by my gathering up the hapless daisy that another ranger's foot had separated from its stalk. Even heathens know it's against the law actually to *pick* a flower inside a park, but I truly didn't see any harm in *picking up* one that had just been trampled down by a lug-soled leather boot. When that daisy landed behind my ear, though, I found myself holding a ticket for instant admission to an evangelical sermon: "The Human's Proper Place in Nature." *Elsewhere* seemed to be the only proper place—a moral gleaned directly from fellow environmentalists who see humans as being somehow unnatural. Nothing in my life to that moment had prepared me for that sermon. Leaving wasn't possible: I was married to a ranger whom I respected, and he agreed with the preacher on this daisy question. Besides, I had nowhere else to go, so I dropped the flower.

Having been raised on a farm with little-n nature all about—an integral and usually unremarked part of daily existence—I was rather slow to comprehend the significance of big-N Nature. For one thing, I was unprepared for how alienated Nature was from people, how separate from everyday life things like birds and chipmunks were inside National Park Service boundaries. Suddenly it was wrong to leave sandwich crumbs for the little ones after a meal—Mammaw Ruth's stern reminders that it was rude to eat in front of the animals without sharing with them were abruptly confronted by the knowledge that sharing with the animals inside a National Park was illegal and deserved a ticket. I soon became a determinedly rude human being in the Park Service, cleaning up even the tiniest crumb before leaving a lunch site and advising other humans to observe the same behavior, as we proved by our actions how disconnected our species was from all others.

Utterly lost without having yet noticed it, I set out to *learn* Nature—to master all the details of this now alien world about me that formerly I'd either ignored or simply appreciated. Latin names, growing seasons, mating rituals, bird calls, scat qualities, geological facts . . . suddenly everything needed *knowing*, not because existence required it, but because it was embarrassing not to know these basics when surrounded by people who had the functional equivalent of a Ph.D. in Nature. But this road to knowledge, this business of running in circles after the Nature-Facts Phantom, risks making one's lost situation permanent.

Hindsight is not only twenty-twenty; it operates as a sixth sense sometimes. Put bluntly, though I would have vehemently denied it back then, I began cultivating in myself some of the traits I liked least about the sermonizers: collecting knowledge and experience of the natural environment, wrapping it like a cloak around my ignorance, and wearing it far too many days in a row without washing it. Some of my new colleagues ridiculed anything southern (especially my accent) or agricultural (even small farms like the one I grew up on), so I learned not to mention my roots in the South, where things like horses and pigs and electric storms had kept my knowledge about nature from outrunning my common sense. Still humble about anything I didn't know adequately (pretty much everything but wildflowers and introduced species), I eventually managed to feel downright arrogant about the Latin names of flowering desert plants.

One morning, after hearing a park superintendent misidentify a cactus and then later proceed to tell a couple visitors that the (non-native) tamarisk was "as indigenous as the Indians," I even grumbled to Frank, "All these employees who can't be bothered to learn anything about Nature ought to be fired—they've got no business managing our natural resources." Nature had become a proper noun to me by then, and somewhere along the way I had begun to think I knew how people ought to act in it too. On another afternoon, when a testy tourist yelled at me, threatening to sue the Park Service because he couldn't see any *real* flowers in the Monument—even though the ground was carpeted with wildflowers in every direction—I suggested tartly that he drive on to Los Angeles and find a funeral home, since it would surely have plenty of roses, and thought to myself as he stormed off that roses might be recognizable flowers, but they looked and smelled like hell.

I began this book by saying that time can jostle us loose from even the most perverse origins. Given enough opportunity, it also can snatch us back from the yawning jaws of our own stupidity by reconnecting us with the parts of our pasts that were not at all perverse, the parts that need remembering and valuing. That process can be a slow one, though, and time is not a commodity in ample supply when you're not sure where you are. Perhaps some people only get slightly disoriented when they step off the trail, but let me get one foot headed in the wrong direction and I can wind up completely lost three steps later.

It's always the little things, the tiny decisions or nondecisions, that contribute most to losing one's way. In the environmental arm of the Park Service I often felt like a freshwater fish that had been dumped into the Dead Sea. Yet that in itself was not sufficient reason to panic and start flapping spastically, periodically tossing out yet another of my core values because the salt was stinging my eyes. Flinging overboard everything I was could not make the water one whit less salty, nor would it effect a biological miracle: My gills did not suddenly develop the ability to process salt water. Nor did mimicking my associates' behavior and mannerisms help. They were accustomed to that place— acclimated to it, perhaps—and I wasn't.

But that's hindsight, at least part of which began evolving when I started tracking. Wandering about the desert looking hard at the ground, I had little time and less inclination to worry about the latest academic quarrels over plant classifications or resource management decisions. Tracking yanked me out of Nature and eventually dropped me back into the heart of nature with a little n.

Tracking requires more than merely learning to read signs on the ground. You have to learn to read people too. And that means you can't get your back up every time some loudmouthed man complains because he can't find roses in the desert. Nor can you walk off and dismiss park superintendents who authoritatively give out wrong information. Arrogance is an utterly useless trait for a tracker. Far better to learn to listen to everything and everyone for a while first, a technique somewhat akin to floating on your back in a salty sea. Suspended there, you learn to appreciate this place and its inhabitants for what they are. You begin to value their existence, and to see the small miracles in their different adaptive mechanisms. After all, little-n nature requires diversity. Again, that's hindsight.

Perhaps it's time to admit that if trackers didn't pay attention to hindsight, they'd be as lost as guppies on a tree branch. The track on the ground conveys skeletal information. It's up to your mind and eyes to remember backward and sideways enough to put that skimpy data into an active alliance with footprints past. If trackers couldn't manage that simple task, there wouldn't be much point in them looking for anyone else who was lost—there'd just be an extra person fumbling around in the vicinity. Looking backward and sideways while keeping your eyes focused forward is a crucial part of knowing not just where you are—but also where the one you seek may be.

One of the most significant functions of hindsight is its ability to prepare you for abrupt shifts in direction. When you're looking forward, behind, and to the sides simultaneously, a ninety-degree turn to the left is almost predictable. So is a 180 to the right. But even if neither was entirely anticipated, they certainly won't have been a surprise: You may still trip and fall, but you shouldn't land flat on your face. That's one of the loveliest gifts of hindsight.

The Park Service was one of my teachers in Joshua Tree. Time spent alone in the desert—time spent becoming a tracker—was another. These two ways of being ran parallel to one another for quite some time, but eventually the lessons I learned from each of them began to diverge. What the desert was teaching me flatly contradicted several of the National Park Service's givens.

Signs on the ground. A novice learning to track. Try it for yourself. Pretend you're in the desert and walk across a sandbox. Then turn around and look at your footprints. Move to a patch of dirt and do the same thing. Now try it across gravel. Grass, freshly mowed. Grass that has never seen a lawnmower and never will. A pile of fall leaves. Moss along a forest path. A creek bank. Now walk through mud onto a sidewalk or street. Then through sand onto the street. Try grass to the street. And don't forget to keep looking back at your tracks.

On some of these surfaces, you'll see your own footprints as clearly as if they'd just been painted there in fire-engine red. But on others, it will seem as if you had walked on air as you came over. While fire-engine red is easier, faster tracking, the walking on air is much more fun and challenging. Here your eyes and brain and intuition must take over.

Look for patterns. Let those three words percolate in your head and look for whatever is not random. Gazing across a stretch of undisturbed ground, you will notice that its soil, sand, stones, and sticks lie together almost haphazardly. Unless some type of movement has occurred there, the ground surface will appear random to the human eye. There may be more stones in one area than another, fewer sticks under one bush than the one twenty yards away, more sand drifted up against one side of a cutbank than the other, and almost no soil on some rock surfaces while others are completely covered. But despite all these differences, undisturbed ground reveals itself as untraversed, patternless.

Since evidence of movement is what the tracker must find first, patterns are crucial. Patterns often mean people. And people can't fly. Patterns can also mean ants, bugs, rabbits, coyotes, dogs, deer, or burros, but you're not likely to mistake any of their tracks for those of humans—unless you're in a very big hurry or doing more birdwatching than tracking. As you already know, I'm not easily distracted by birds (they all look vaguely alike to me anyway), so my eyes tend to stay riveted to the ground.

"Patterns" is a vague sort of word. So what *are* you looking for? Well, full tracks or imprints of your shoe soles are nice. But failing that, impressions. Broken twigs. Bent grass. Shiny surfaces. Grains of dirt left on top of a stick. Maybe the stick has made a slightly darker impression on the ground underneath it (which means somebody stepped on it). Crushed rabbit pellets. Scuff marks. Pebbles pressed into the soil—not by time, by a foot, so you look for loosening at an edge that might mean the pressing was more recent than last year's last flash flood. Coloration changes—when a stone or leaf or stick has been turned over, there'll often be a difference in shade from the ones that haven't been disturbed. Anything that isn't random. There, see? You're tracking. Following your own signs backward.

To get any good at this, you'd have to set this book aside and track for hours, even days. Nothing can teach you to track if you are not willing to put in dirt time. Solitary time. No distractions, no breaks, no visiting. Hundreds of hours of just you out there following whatever tracks you can find as far as you can follow them in all kinds of weather and light conditions. You have to follow ants and kangaroo rats, little kids and old people, bighorn sheep and coyotes, runners and skiers, rattlesnakes and lizards. Follow them to their homes or their watering holes or their stalking spots. Learn to recognize the marks they leave on grasses and sand as they pass.

Step on branches or grass yourself, memorize the spot, and come back thirty days in a row to watch the coloration changes a plant goes through when healing itself. Forget about describing it to anyone else: The English language has no words precise enough to characterize the subtleties of shade that you will see. What counts is that you perceive the changes and let your eyes and mind remember them for you. Vegetation healing rates not only give crude information (someone stepped on this branch); they can also help you to figure the age of a track with reasonable accuracy (someone stepped on this branch more than twenty-four hours and less than three days ago). But healing occurs at different tempos for different plants, even if the same amount of pressure is applied to them all, and weather conditions make a crucial difference too. So a grass stem that normally returns to its upright position six hours after being lightly stepped on may still be lying flat two days later if there has been low humidity and no breeze at all. Conversely, if rain fell after you stepped on the grass, it may be standing upright in a matter of minutes. Both wind and water, in even the most minuscule amounts, affect vegetation healing rates and track decomposition. And sometimes plants aren't damaged at all by footsteps—they're just lying where the shoe left them for the time being, so the term "healing rate" itself isn't even entirely accurate.

To become a tracker, then, you have to learn to read subtle changes in signs for which you will normally have no descriptive language. You must rely solely on your own patience, determination, and six senses—sight, hearing, smell, touch, taste, and intuition. There is no quick, five-step method for becoming a tracker (tracking weekends with the "experts" notwithstanding). No one else can teach you to track, no matter how much money you pay them or how much time you spend with them. Until you put in enough dirt time yourself, you cannot follow footprints on the ground.

Late August, 1986
Cottonwood Ranger Station

Today Ruthie came home.

After several months of having Kevin say one day that he was sending the kids out to live with us, and then the very next day swear I would never see either of them again, Ruthie's arrival here was too sudden to seem real. The few minutes I had to hold both my children in my arms passed swiftly, ending with Kevin saying that he had decided to keep Jon because "he's much less trouble than his sister." I watched my son walk away with his father while holding my daughter close and crying tears of both grief and joy. Thinking of Jonathan sends sharp pains through my body, fire racing along nerve endings, but I will not let the grief spill onto Ruthie. She needs to feel safe here.

I am too excited and tense to sleep, so I just lie here on the bed watching my daughter doze off in her new room. Her hair has gotten darker and longer over the last year, and her skin is brown as a hickory nut—the way it always is in the summer. She stirs often and calls for me, small fingers gripping my shirt or hand tightly for a few minutes before falling asleep again. I sing her favorite song every time she wakes, crying silently on the last line every time.

> You are my sunshine, my only sunshine.
> You make me happy when skies are grey.
> You'll never know, dear, how much I love you.
> Please don't take my sunshine away.

This evening before dark Ruthie walked in the desert with me, both of us pausing every few steps for another hug or close perusal of something small: a beetle, a horned toad, and a young chuckwalla; one dove, two roadrunners, and a whole covey of quail; a grey and pink rock; two dried desert birdcages and ten desert trumpet stems; one spider's web and three spiders; and too many plants to count. Ruthie loves the flora here.

She stopped in midstep on glimpsing her first cactus. "What's *that?*" she asked, head turned slightly to one side, staring wide-eyed at the prickly plant.

"It's a cactus—one of the opuntia," I replied.

"O-what?"

"Opuntia is the name of its family. *Opuntia ramosissima.*"

"But Mommy, what's its *pretty* name?"

"Cholla—actually, I think pencil cholla is what most people call it."

Ruthie nodded approvingly and said, "It *looks* like a lot of little pencils stuck everywhere with pins!"

And as we walked away, several minutes later, she commented, "I sure do like those pretty names, Mommy."

As my daughter rouses from sleep yet again, this time to look into my eyes and ask a question—"Will Jonny come home again?"—I remember her last words near the cactus a few hours ago. "Jonny would like the pretty names too."

Drifting off to sleep, I vow to leave the Latin names for plants to biologists and rangers and folks who need them. From today, I will use the common—or, as my daughter would put it, the pretty—names. That way I'll know them when my son comes again.

POINT LAST SEEN

NOBODY GOES ANYWHERE without leaving signs on the ground, a small fact of enormous significance for trackers. As is common in most activities, starting points are critical. In search and rescue, the single place of greatest potential use is the point last seen (PLS). When you're trying to locate a missing person, the place where he or she was last seen is vitally important territory. Getting to that location before all signs of the lost person have been trampled or otherwise destroyed often is the tracker's first priority on any search. It's there, at the PLS, that you can usually find some of the best clues.

FEBRUARY 1986
JACKSON HOLE TO JOSHUA TREE

Why does an otherwise sane woman choose to move from the resplendent Grand Tetons to the bottom of the Mojave Desert, anyway? I ask myself that question late this afternoon as I drive from Amboy, California, toward Twentynine Palms. Jackson Hole is twelve hundred miles behind me, our old Mission 66 house is buried in snow up to the tops of its windows, Frank is driving the FourRunner just ahead, and the only houses I have seen for miles are ramshackle cabins with broken windows and rotted frames. Waning sunlight, which in Wyoming produces splendid alpenglow on the Teton mountains, only makes this tawdry, deserted land look flatter and less appealing by the mile.

"We *requested* this transfer," I keep saying to myself, hands firmly on the steering wheel and eyes forward in an attempt to ignore the bleak expanses on either side of the car. "We *wanted* to move to the desert," my brain adds. But that was when I thought it all looked like Death Valley or Ely.

"Why didn't we visit before we agreed to come here?" I say into the CB radio.

Frank, laughing in the vehicle up ahead, just says, "It'll be better when we reach the Monument. Are you getting tired?"

"No, just questioning my sanity at the moment—yours too. Have you taken a good look out the windows lately?"

After a long silence, Frank's voice, sounding subdued and pensive, replies, "Yeah, it sure looks like a lot of people come here and leave, doesn't it?"

There ought to be a law that says people have to take all their trash when they go, not leave it standing there on the sand to dryrot for the next century. Broken glass, scattered beer cans and fifty-gallon drums, old newspapers and McDonald's wrappers, abandoned cars riddled with bullet holes, vulgar graffiti on rocks and road signs and the walls of empty houses, a few people who look at you as if you're a serial killer when you wave so you stop doing that after a few miles. So this is California. We just passed a sign that said "Welcome to Wonder Valley." I wonder who ever came up with that name.

That night found us ensconced in a gaudily decorated hotel room on the edge of town. I dozed off thinking about a dawn so clear that breathing hurt, reassured that this desert dawn was only a few hours of coral and lime green sleep away. At Cotton-wood, I promised myself, we'll watch the sun rise and forget about Wonder Valley, and maybe I'll regain some perspective on California.

Next morning we overslept.

Perspective regularly eludes humans in southern California, largely because it is so hard to avoid gut-wrenching extremes there. Try driving from Wonder Valley through Joshua Tree Na-tional Monument and ending your day in Palm Springs. Acres of green grass, dotted with weeping willows and flamingos and waterpools, grace the city's walled communities—overwatered landscaping that says that all it takes to make the desert bloom is a little vision, work, and a great deal of money and water.

Had I seen Palm Springs during the first few days after arriving in California, I would have headed back to Wyoming on the spot. But since I didn't venture down out of the Monument for two months, my disenchantment with the state was only gradual. At the end of it, I had utterly surrendered myself to Nature and had come to think of the Monument's Cottonwood district as the one safe place for me in southern California. I began to spend more and more time alone in the desert learning to track.

Sometimes the lessons we learn are so gradual that it seems as if the answers lay within us all along. Some of them may well have done so. But many more, I think, lie in those indistinct signs on the ground that we can hardly see. Too frequently we notice vague signs, hesitate, and miss the lesson entirely. How many lessons can we miss before we've jeopardized the whole search?

LATE MARCH 1986
PALM SPRINGS, CALIFORNIA

A trip down Palm Canyon Drive in broad daylight during spring break is a sojourn in a foreign country. Here all the natives have dark tans; wear outrageously trendy clothes set off with bangles, beads, huge sunglasses, and even larger diamond rings, gold watches, and bracelets; and sport unwrinkled faces (even if those faces have been atop those necks for eighty years). Theatrical-grade makeup and eyelashes are liable to appear on both men and women; every third voice gushes in Zsa Zsa's "Dahling" tones; and an utterly affected accent suffuses all conversation. The younger people are simply more animated versions of their elders. Arm in arm, they stroll together, vivacious laughter brimming from unnaturally white smiles. As an awed observer on her first visit, I tried hard not to stare, to act as if these few blocks of concrete and blistering sunshine and noise were my normal stomping grounds—after all, I'd just spent the last few weeks living at an isolated ranger station in the desert without even a telephone, so it was high time to visit Palm Springs. Only obstinacy kept me from beating a hasty retreat.

I walked down the sidewalk in a daze, jostled by people moving in all directions, people who were giving every impression of having the time of their lives. Even the sunlight was oppressive, ricocheting off a store window or the splendid white calla lilies on a woman's hat; the noise, suffocating, blaring upward from car engines and horns and radios, outward from hundreds of human mouths. Bound inside an invisible bubble of ear splitting sound, I could hardly breathe. Coming here was clearly a mistake (for once, "When in Rome, do as the Romans do" seemed the most vapid statement in human history). Then, thankfully, I was rescued by a bookstore.

From the refuge of the store, standing well back from its front windows, I looked out on the teeming street. Where are all the poor people? Or, for that matter, the *ordinary* people? Are they out there? Maybe so. Maybe when people come to Palm Springs they just look and act like this, sort of like visiting Vegas, then they go home and dress and behave normally—probably wouldn't even recognize them back in their hometowns. Unconvinced by my lame reasoning, I retreated further into the cool, dimly lit room.

Book jackets are endlessly compelling even when you don't have much money, but you can hide in a bookstore only so long before you have to go back outside and face the music— in this case, the din—of reality. I bought a Wallace Stegner paperback (in it was sure to be a world I knew and cherished), then opened the door and resolutely headed for my car, clutching the book like a shield in front of me. At the very first intersection, a haggard-looking woman pushing a grocery cart full of paper bags stuffed with old clothes stopped in front of me, waiting to cross. Sitting on top of the bags was a little girl no more than two years old whose huge searching eyes caught and held mine for a moment. Here are the poor people you were wondering about, I thought.

The light changed, stopping the traffic in front of us, and a huge white Rolls Royce purred to a stop, silhouetting the woman and the little girl. I didn't have even a dollar bill in my pocket; I'd spent all the money I'd brought on that damned book. Nauseated by how much my own self-centeredness seemed of a piece with that of the people around me, I ran across the intersection, dodging white-toothed people left and right. It took me twenty minutes to reach my car and throw the book in the back seat, and another thirty to get out of Palm Springs, but I arrived home before dark. Never had a stretch of unirrigated land looked more appealing to me than Joshua Tree National Monument did that evening.

Arid places do not absolve guilt or even assuage it, but they do provide space for reflection. That night I sat and thought a long time about the ways in which my own behavior was complicit in all the hunger and suffering in our world. Knowing that I was only a few months beyond being just as gaunt and homeless as that woman on the street, the money I had spent on Stegner's book burned deep shame inside me. Sixteen dollars. One damned book or twelve gallons of milk. Three hundred pages that I could have checked out of a library or four packages of bologna, three loaves of bread, eight apples, and six oranges. There might even have been enough money left for the woman to buy her child some M&M's. The little girl's eyes had looked just like Ruthie's, wide, questioning, and all too knowing. Quiet, brown, melancholy eyes like my own daughter's that probably no longer dared cry for mommy.

That Stegner book remains unopened even now, years after its purchase. Somehow I've always figured its author would understand why without having to be told. Today, many deliberate visits to Palm Springs later, where I've walked up and down Palm Canyon Drive watching the people and trying to figure out what makes them tick, I still haven't managed to leave the place once without quiet sadness. But I've finally learned that I can no longer escape Palm Springs or Wonder Valley by going to a place like Joshua Tree. They are all cut from the same piece of cloth.

Part of the process of getting lost is losing sight of your reference points without noticing they have disappeared. Then when your memory tries to connect itself to something familiar, it's gone— so blunt senses, accessed by feet or eyes or noses, readily mislead. And once your memory has been compromised, it is likely to deceive you further. You may know that on some deep level, but accepting it might well turn out to be one of the hardest things you've ever tried to do. And reversing the trend of a compromised memory may be well nigh impossible.

AUGUST 1988
Kevin has let Jonathan spend half the summer with Frank, Ruthie, and me at Cottonwood. Ruthie was right: her brother loves the common names for plants, but he likes the Latin names too and (much to his sister's dismay) has quickly begun hyphenating scientific and pretty names. Our days for the last few weeks have been full of playing hide-and-seek with our dog Sam, hik-

ing desert canyons, rock climbing, and camping out in our backyard. Our nights echo those that followed Ruthie's arrival here a year ago: Jon often wakes up screaming several times a night, with such horrible nightmares that he cannot even tell us what they are. When he realizes where he is, he holds on to me tightly and gets very quiet, but sometimes it takes hours before he actually goes back to sleep.

Yesterday we received a letter from Kevin, saying he wanted to take Ruthie and Jon on vacation, but that he'd then like to bring them both back to live with Frank and me because he had decided to remarry. No one in this house had a nightmare last night, but I lay awake all night anyway, listening to the quiet, praying that this time things would be different, begging for my children's safety, wanting to take them and run away so that there would be no chance that anyone could hurt them again, trying hard to believe Kevin's assurances that he had changed and could be trusted.

SEPTEMBER 1988

For three days now Kevin has called and left instructions for Frank and me to meet him to pick up the children, but he has never shown up. Today he called and said that he would only let me have Jon and Ruthie if I would agree to meet him in the desert alone. I am tortured by the need for my children, but I know I cannot say yes without risking their lives and mine.

Five days ago, shortly after Kevin left his house with the children, his girlfriend called Frank and me. Introducing herself, she said that Kevin had packed a whole suitcase of guns and left promising to take care of me "once and for all."

"Whatever you do," she said, "Don't meet him alone in the desert."

She was moving out, trying to get away before Kevin came home, afraid for her life, yet feeling guilty that she would no longer be around to watch out for Ruthie and Jon—"He has not hurt them in my presence," she said, "but I know he does when I'm not here."

Before hanging up, she said, "I don't know you, but I know what your children say about you, and I had to warn you."

A woman I'd never met was now in almost the same situation with Kevin that I'd been in for years—and she was calling to warn me. We talked for a long time, two women connected by a phone line and our fear of one man and of the justice system that allowed him to brutalize women and children at will.

Stay alive. Not for yourself, but for those children. Stay strong. Do not let him get the three of you in one place, for then he will follow through on his plans: to torture your children and make you watch as they die. He has been planning this a long time. Other than the suitcase-full-of-guns part, she was telling me nothing I did not already know.

In his last phone call, Kevin repeated his demand that I meet him alone in the desert. "That's the only way you can prove you trust me—and the only way you'll get to see your kids again."

"I will not meet you alone," I said, drained of all feeling.

"Then your kids will always know that you didn't love them or want them there after all—isn't that right, kids?" he said, as Ruthie cried out in the background, and then the line went dead and my children disappeared from my life again.

This time I went to the desert's mountains, walking through the pain day after day, alternating between hope and fear, rage and hopelessness. But this time I was present with different feet. Having once seen and chuckled at a chuckwalla's antics with Ruthie, I could not walk past the lizard's territory without looking for him and feeling my daughter's presence. Having once climbed a certain rock face in the canyon with Jon, I could not pass it again without seeing my son grinning his way to the top. Having spent the last fall helping Ruthie get through her nightmares—and most of the summer doing the same with Jon—I could not find sleep, knowing that my children were once more living their nightmares, day and night. Faith was no longer a possibility, for no God could exist in a world this cruel to its progeny. Putting one foot in front of another was my only alternative: tracking to stay alive, not daring to think beyond each moment, forcing myself not to see Ruth's slightly turned-out, sturdy footprints or Jon's flat-footed tracks everywhere we had been. For a while I gratefully hid inside the National Park Service's Nature, trying to get together enough money to hire a lawyer to help bring Jon and Ruth home.

It is difficult not to idealize Joshua Tree National Monument when you've driven through the desert from Amboy to Twentynine Palms or walked down Palm Canyon Drive in broad daylight. The emptiness of desert air quickly dissipates wounded human feelings, and the vast expanses of unpeopled land can offer a fast, convincing antidote to human society. Realization that the peace is only superficial, a placebo at best, comes much later, if at all.

When Kevin took Jon and Ruthie away that summer, I walked and tracked a lot, but spent little or no time considering the implications of what I was doing. Without my children, thinking was a sad business, so I gradually became the best version of a Nature lover that I could without really wondering why. The desert welcomed me, day or night, and gave me a safe, quiet place to retreat: that it deserved protection from the ravages of "unnatural" humans was undeniable—and its own "naturalness" invited no reflection anyway. But learning to track meant that I eventually did a lot of reflecting on my feet. And the further I went with tracking, the harder it became for me to wear the garb of the truly redeemed Nature lover. Despite its solitude, dirt time was too fundamentally *cultural*—about *people*—for me to accept their "unnaturalness" for long.

Nature can't save a pragmatic soul from herself. No matter how much she may try, someone like me who was raised on a working farm can never get very far from working on the land. Which is precisely what tracking is: a job that forces you to get down on the ground, to put in dirt time, to get some dust in your eyes and some sweat on your body, and to experience places like the desert firsthand—not for a brief viewing visit, but for long enough that you feel the screams of the land itself and of the many species who live on it .

"Screams of the land" talk makes some people nervous, and I'll admit that it sounds a little overwrought. But try watching a tourist swerve ten feet out of his lane to hit a red diamond rattlesnake that has just crossed the road in front of him. Run over to that snake as the four-wheel-drive speeds off and see that she was probably within a few hours at most of having babies. Watch her writhing, unable to die quickly unless you help with a strong blow to her head. Try walking into an illegal campsite and finding a desert tortoise skewered with sharpened sticks. Not killed for food, just tortured for fun and left to die, its eyes watching the ranger approach—once again to deliver the final blow. Try doing these things on a regular enough basis until you can hear the land scream. If it doesn't, you surely will be. Maybe that *is* a bit overwrought—maybe it should be.

—

Try following any set of footprints long enough that you start to care about the existence of the one who made the tracks: Animal or human, the one she follows matters as much to the tracker as her own existence. After a few months of tracking, I developed a quirky gait which persists even now, the result of trying to avoid stepping on even the tiniest, most "inconsequential" beings: ants, for example. To spear a tortoise for fun or deliberately run over a snake—what benefit does one possibly obtain from such violence and cruelty? Seeing these things while I was working close to the land and its nonhuman creatures helped me to appreciate the notion of big-N Nature even as I ultimately rejected it for myself. When I remember some of the things Park Service employees and other environmentalists are trying to combat, when I remind myself that they are trying to prevent places like Joshua Tree from becoming Palm Springs or Wonder Valley, I too want to put a fence around Nature to protect it from the violence of the human species.

—

Much of what I learned about tracking was gleaned straight from the desert. Training seminars in the Park Service, usually conducted by specific volunteer rescue groups with tracking expertise, were largely practice sessions for beginners. During my first tracking weekend I sat indoors for about eight hours the first day. I spent one third of that time listening to two tracking "experts" argue over terminology: "stride" vs. "step interval." In any set of tracks, the "stride" is the distance from the heel of the back foot to the heel of the front foot, the first man said. But "step interval," said the second man, the distance between the front of the back foot and the back of the front foot, is a more appropriate measure for trackers to use in the field. While they argued I sat doodling on my notebook, wondering why we couldn't all just agree to be precise about both terms and use whichever one we preferred in the field. Two hours later, with both men still arguing for standardizing their particular word choice, someone in the audience wearily suggested that perhaps we should all just agree to be precise about both terms and use whichever one we preferred in the field. After another half hour of disagreement, the experts reluctantly agreed, then one of them suggested that we break for lunch.

The first hour of that afternoon was devoted to statistical search probabilities. Another expert was trying to develop a computer program for predicting a lost person's rate and direction of travel. Young children and old people were more likely than young adults to take the path of least resistance—for example, to go downhill instead of up if given the choice. Questions flooded my head: But most kids love to climb rocks, don't they? (Jon sure does.) And if they're following a lizard or a rabbit will they even notice they're going up? (Ruthie wouldn't.) So is this a chronological age and inclination thing or a physical fitness thing? Do old people necessarily avoid hills? (What if they're in good shape and would like to see the view from that out- cropping?) Don't even fit young adults get tired sometimes and choose the easiest path? (I sure do.) What about things like de- pression or hiking experience or anger or fear? (Don't they all matter greatly when someone decides to take a hike and then gets lost?) How can you possibly factor these unquantifiable in- fluences into a computer program?

What about topography? Would not terrain play a role here? Where did the statistics for these models come from? Given how sketchy most search records are, how could the data ever suffice for predictive modeling? Is there really any way to predict one human's behavior from someone else's somewhere else if the two shared nothing more than chronological age and the temporary state of "lostness"? The key claim of the presentation was that computers were on the verge of helping SAR trackers "get inside the head" of the lost person more effectively than had ever been possible—even for the world-renowned Bushman trackers of Africa. "Getting inside the head" meant that trackers practically didn't have to follow footprints anymore: they could "mind-track" instead. (*Mind*-track? Get real.) That first tracking seminar was a very long weekend indeed.

The desert is full of places that fall squarely between the opposed poles of Wonder Valley/Palm Springs and Joshua Tree National Monument. Chiriaco Summit, a small truckstop outside the south boundary of the park, is one such place. Hot, human, noisy, and often smelly, its tumble of buildings—gas station, cafe, General Patton museum, post office window, motel, cactus garden, and trailer houses—stand in stark contrast to the tranquility of the surrounding desert.

The first time I walked into Chiriaco Summit, I was hot and tired from having spent most of the morning volunteering for the Park Service. I wanted a rootbeer float pretty badly or I'd have just hurried back into the sanctuary of Park Service space. Frank and I ordered, and ten minutes later the waitress returned with my float.

She firmly set a brown plastic glass of ice cream on the table in front of me; put an unopened can of off-brand rootbeer next to it; dropped a spoon, straw, and napkin next to the can; and turned around and walked off without so much as a word. My "thank you" seemed to have gone unheard.

I looked first at the plastic glass and the can, then up at Frank. Within seconds we were both laughing so hard I could hardly fix my float. We went to Chiriaco Summit many times afterward— every time we needed to use a phone or mail a letter, and any time we needed a float and a laugh—and I gradually learned to appreciate this quirky human place for what it was.

WALKING THE PERIMETER

HAVING A PLS is no guarantee that searchers will suddenly find a set of tracks leading them straight to the lost person. Usually the situation is far less clear-cut: There may be thirty sets of footprints, eighteen of which may be the same size as the lost person's. Or there may be twenty-four sets of adult tracks present and not a single kid's—who, of course, is the one that's lost. Or, as was the case with the child who went missing on my first real search, the tracker might have a shoe size and good description of the sole, but find ten or twelve different sets of prints from the lost person crisscrossing the area. To figure out where the lost person *is*, you have to step back—literally—and walk the perimeter, cutting for sign as you go.

SAR trackers do this not just around the PLS, but whenever they need to restart a track. Some of us cut sign out of habit any time we go anywhere: When walking outdoors, I almost instinctively notice whatever signs cross my path—footprints of beetles, coyotes, cats, the neighbor lady from two houses down. This practice isn't as ridiculous as it sounds, for when I need to look for one particular person, my mind simply starts a filtering process on all the tracks I see, watching for any place those two lost feet may have intersected my path, looking for clues that will bring me alongside those unique tracks.

———

Living at a remote desert ranger station in a National Monument means that every time a stranger knocks on your door there's trouble. Visitors never stop by just to say what a wonderful trip they're having or to ask if you've seen the cactus wrens nesting at Campsite 68. Perhaps they're deterred by the prominent Private/Residents Only signs. These signs, however, make no impression whatsoever on a visitor in trouble, potential or real. So every knock on the door heralds a problem that rangers or their families are supposed to be able to fix: a rattlesnake is holed up in the ladies' restroom at the campground; a coyote ran across the road just inside the entrance gates, causing a three-car accident; a visitor first backed up against, then fell headlong into, a cholla cactus family; a climber fell off a rock wall; a Ford Escort is stuck in deep sand on an unmaintained off-road-vehicles-only road.

If some of the reasons visitors have for knocking on the door are humorous, one is never funny: someone is missing. Without a great deal of luck or knowledge, a lost person will not last long in the desert. (Climbing accidents technically aren't funny either, but it's not unusual for downed climbers, if conscious, to make wisecracks about their situation.) Lost people quite often come from cities, where they navigate by street signs and walk on sidewalks, and they have no idea how easy it is to get off a supposedly "marked" trail and how hard it can be to get back on again. The lost person often first arrives in the park with a group—Boy Scouts or Marines or a family—but then for some reason winds up alone and disoriented. Perhaps an apparent shortcut made it seem likely that she would be able to beat everybody else back to camp. Or maybe the group pace was too fast for him. One child might have seen a rabbit disappear into the bush, while another simply got tired. An adult in a tiresome relationship may even choose to "get lost." Whatever the reasons, they are far from idiosyncratic.

Simply *getting* lost doesn't necessarily pose a problem, because with clear thinking one's steps can be retraced fairly quickly. But clear thinking is usually the first trait to go when someone looks around and sees nothing at all that is familiar. Hurried movement, instinctive as it may be, compounds the trouble. And considering the desert fashions that some visitors favor (bikinis, sandals, no hat) and their lack of preparation (failure to bring water or sunscreen, for instance), the survival of anyone who steps off the trail and gets lost in the Mojave Desert may be immediately threatened. Contrary to folklore, coaxing potable drinking water from a barrel cactus is all but impossible without a chainsaw. Hot daytime temperatures, which suck moisture out of the body at noon, plummet at dusk, summoning hypothermia. Cactus, snakes, and rough terrain easily become serious hazards when you are tired, hungry, and thirsty, cold or hot, and above all frightened. And where a lost child is concerned, abduction is always a possibility. For the tracker, who is often one of dozens of searchers, every move is grimly dogged by the knowledge that success or failure may equal life or death for the lost person.

Hollywood and outdoor magazines have given us an image of search and rescue as glamorous and macho, but in a real-world search, tracking is hard, dirty, and sometimes terribly disappointing work. And then along comes a search where everything goes right by the book—and the tracking team you're on makes a fast, exhilarating find. Nothing feels much better than finding someone still alive.

MAY 1986
COTTONWOOD DISTRICT,
JOSHUA TREE NATIONAL MONUMENT

My first actual search began while I was still sound asleep, sometime near dawn one morning when a nine-year-old girl named Mandy Evans went to the restroom at Cottonwood Campground and did not return to her parents' campsite. Less than half a mile away, I got up, stretched, went for a short run with Sam, showered, ate breakfast, and dressed for work—a world away from and completely oblivious to the commotion at the campground, where campers of all ages were frantically searching for Mandy. For me, the only tracker in that part of Joshua Tree that morning, the search didn't start until her worried father knocked on our door—long after the herd of concerned campers had tramped and backtramped all over Loop B, where Mandy had last been seen. Looking for her, in good-neighborly fashion, they had unwittingly complicated our best chance of finding her quickly—or at all.

The knock came at 7:55 A.M., exactly one minute before I would've left the house for volunteer naturalist work at the Cottonwood Visitor Center. Frank immediately began a lost persons report, and I was out of the house with my search pack less than five minutes later.

0800 hours, Cottonwood Campground, Loop B

Getting this campsite and restroom area cordoned off is my first concern right now. Mandy's tracks should be everywhere—she's been playing around her parents' camper for two days—but the more people that walk through here, the tougher it will be to figure out where she's gone. I'm stringing bright orange fluorescent tape around the campsite now.

"Here it is!" Mandy's mom calls out from the camper. She's found a tee shirt we can use for a scent article if necessary.

"Great!" I call back (hoping she hasn't forgotten already and touched the shirt) and add another reminder, "Remember, don't let *any*body at all touch it, okay? I'm going to cordon off the restroom and then I'll be back here to look for prints." To Mandy's sister I say, "Lisa, it sure would help me a lot if you'd tell people not to walk through here right now—think you could do that for me?"

She crosses her arms grimly and says, "I sure *can*." (I wouldn't want to be the first adult that tries to step over that orange tape.)

0815

"Tracker One to Base," I say into my radio while walking back toward Mandy's campsite.

"Go ahead, One." It's Frank, so he's still manning the radio.

"Campsite 12 and the Loop B restroom are both cordoned off. We have a scent article at the camper, and I'm on my way back to see if I can isolate Mandy's tracks. Can you get some more trackers in here to help? One over."

"Riverside Mountain Rescue Unit is on standby—I'll call them in and bring Skip down from topside to help 'til they can get here. Let me know if you need anybody else. Base over."

"We've still got cars going in and out of this campground right and left—need to shut down the road at the entrance stat—is Al free to do that 'til we can get a law enforcement ranger down here? One over."

"Base copy. Al's already on his way down now, and I'm working on getting RSO [Riverside Sheriff's Office] deputies or BLM [Bureau of Land Management] to check cars leaving the south entrance. Topside is sending two rangers, ETA forty-five minutes. Advise when you have tracks isolated. Base over and out."

"One out."

You're never really "out" on a radio in this area. Since Cottonwood Ranger Station has no phones, we rely exclusively on the radio for communication, which means I hear every transmission Frank's making. You have to tune some of it out—listen only to what matters for your particular assignment.

0825

Mandy's mother is more helpful than a lot of people would be in the same situation. She knows her daughter's shoe size, she knows which shoes are missing from the suitcase Mandy packed for the trip, and she knows her daughter well. She is scared for Mandy, but also concerned that she's imposing on us by asking us to look for her.

As I scan the ground surface of the campsite, she says from the camper door, "She might've just gone to the restroom and then got interested in something on the way back and then couldn't find her way back here—she'll probably turn up in the other loop or something! I'm so sorry for the trouble—"

I cross the campsite to circle several prints that have to belong to Mandy (they're too large to be her sister's and too small to be her Mom's) and say, "Believe me, Mrs. Evans—it's *no* trouble. This is the thing we work and train for all the time. Getting Mandy back here safely is *all* we care about, so don't be worrying about putting us out, okay?"

"All right, I guess so—" She sounds unconvinced.

After marking a couple more tracks, I stop and look directly at Mrs. Evans. "I'm going to follow up your hunch—and your daughter's tracks too. It looks like she left here heading for the restroom, so I'll see if I can pick up where she went from there. There'll probably be some more trackers and rangers in here before too long, so if you'd just stay put and keep people from walking through this area, that'd help a lot."

"All right, we'll do that," she says, putting her arm around Lisa's shoulders.

"And try not to worry—we'll get Mandy back here just as fast as we can," I say, looking into Lisa's worried blue eyes.

Mandy's tracks lead straight to the restroom, but I cannot restart them leaving. Too many other people have been here looking for her this morning.

0835
"Tracker One to Base."

"Go ahead, One." Rita has taken over dispatch now.

"I have tracks isolated and marked at Campsite 12 and have followed them to the restroom but can't restart from here—there's been too much traffic—so I'll head down the campground road and do a perimeter cut of Loop B. Do you have an ETA for Riverside's trackers yet?"

Frank comes on: "They're sending six trackers and four search dog teams, ETA three hours. China Lake's on standby and we're pulling in Dale's chopper. Base over and out."

"One out." Good. We'll soon have a helicopter in the air. We could use some eyes in the sky about now.

"Tracker One, Unit 223." It's Skip coming in on the local channel.

"Go ahead, 223."

"If you want some help on that perimeter cut, my ETA is fifteen minutes. 223 out."

"Sounds good, Skip. I'm heading for the group picnic area now and will work north 'til you get here. Search Base, do you copy? One over and out."

"Base to 223. Skip, you can proceed directly to the campground and have Hannah fill you in on what we've got. Base over and out."

"223 copy and out." This is comforting news. Skip and I did a weekend of formal tracking training at China Lake a few weeks ago. He's great to work with.

0850

Skip's ranger vehicle just pulled into the campground. He parks and meets me at the side of the road. "Here's what we have so far," I say, and he takes notes while I flip through my notebook and fill him in on what I've done.

"Tracker One, Search Base."

"Go ahead, Base."

"Unit 210 just arrived—do you need a third on your team?"

"That sounds good to me, if you can spare him. One out."

"He's on his way, you can brief him there. Base over and out."

Jason will be here in two minutes. He trained at China Lake with Skip and me too. We've got a tracking team at last.

0855

"Damn, Hannah—I didn't expect we'd get to do this for real quite so soon," Skip says.

"Me neither," I reply. "Hi there—am I glad to see you!" I say to Jason, who's walking toward us. "Here's what we've got so far," I add.

Jason replies, "Just show me the track and let's get this over with." He and Skip walk up to the campsite to look at the tracks I marked a while ago, and I continue with my perimeter cut.

"Search Base to Alan."

"Go ahead, Base."

"Unit 217 should be at your location any minute. I need you to report back to base stat—we've got an LZ [landing zone for helicopter] to prepare. Base over and out."

"I copy. 217 is pulling up now and I'm on my way. Al out."

Dale's chopper is on the way in.

0900

Jason and Skip return from the campsite and join me in the brush outside the campground. We fan out, about six feet apart, with Skip closest to the road and me farthest out and start moving north.

"34R1 to 14R1." (That's Frank to the chief ranger.)

"Go ahead, Frank."

"We'll need a fuel truck for the chopper. Can you head one this direction? 34R1 over and out."

"We'll get on it right away. You've got another chopper en route from the Marine Base, ETA twenty-five minutes. They'll be in touch with you when they're over the Eagle Mountains. 14R1 out."

0905

"Hey, come look at this, you two!" Skip calls out. Sure enough, he's got an indistinct footprint the same size as Mandy's. We circle it and move forward slowly til we get a clear print. It's Mandy all right, headed away from the campground.

"Tracker One to Search Base."

"Go ahead, One."

"We've got fresh prints about ten feet off the road just above the Loop B intersection, heading away from the campground, and we're on them."

"Good work, team! Keep us advised. We have two choppers and a fixed wing on the way. ETA on Riverside is two hours. Your new handle will be Tracking Team One."

"Team One copies and is out."

Skip says, "Hannah, since you started all this, why don't you take point first and we'll flank?"

"Well, sure—but you'll both be getting a turn, because this kid has a three- or four-hour head start on us and my eyes'll get sore before too long!"

Skip laughs and says, "Mine are already sore!"

"Mine too—I sure hope this works like it's supposed to, you guys."

"Oh, it'll work just fine," Jason says. "After all, how hard can it be? We just follow the smudges on the ground to the kid, right?"

Something's wrong with Jason, but now's not the time to try to figure out what. "Skip, can you cover the radio?" I ask and we move out.

0930

We were moving fine until three minutes ago. Now we've hit a wide rocky area where we can't see anything but rocks. Mandy had to have crossed here somehow, but I don't see any signs of her. I stand up straight and say, "Damn—she can't have floated, but where did she go? One of you guys want to take point for a while?"

"You're doing just fine, let's just stay with the program: one step at a time," Skip says, echoing our instructors at China Lake. Don't move forward until you've seen the next track.

Crouching down, I look from a different angle. The rocks where Mandy's next foot should've landed look as if they've been in their present positions for fifty years. (I am *really* nervous inside: three green trackers out searching for a lost child?! We must be crazy! I wish the Riverside guys would hurry up and get here.) "We may have to do another perimeter cut on the other side of this," I say, standing up again.

At this, Jason walks up and pushes me aside, saying "I'll take point."

"Great!" I say, relieved to be relieved, and move back to a flanking position.

"Step by step, it's as easy as can be," Jason says and then squats down to look across the rocky stretch for a few seconds. Suddenly he stands up and shouts, "*Nobody* could see tracks on this stuff!"

Skip steps toward him and says, "Let Hannah take point again, Jason."

Jason turns to face Skip and angrily demands, "Think I'm not good enough, do you? Well, I've got news for you—*none* of us is good enough! And even if we were, there isn't *anything* here to see!" Raising his arms, he stomps over Mandy's last track and out into the rocky section, scuffling his feet, and yelling, "See! *Not one damn thing to see!*" Then, pointing at me, "*She's* the only fool who thinks there might be something to see here!"

As Jason starts back toward me, Skip steps forward and takes him by the arm. "C'mon man, back off. We're all doing the best we can do here." I have backed off—*way off*: When men start yelling, my "flight" instinct takes over.

Jason yanks his arm away from Skip's hold and yells, "Why don't you both just admit it: there isn't anything to see here!"

Skip steps toward Jason again and says, "Hey man, let's head back to the entrance. I think Frank probably needs some help with those vehicle searches. Sounds like he needs to send Andy down to the south entrance."

Jason stalks off toward the campground and Skip pats my arm on his way by me, saying quietly, "I'll be back as soon as I can, but I need to get him out of here and settled down—don't worry, you can restart the track and I'll catch up in a few minutes, all right?" And off he goes, leaving me standing there staring wordlessly at Jason's tracks on those rocks.

"Unit 223 to Base." Skip is calling in.

"Go ahead 223."

"Sounds like you need another ranger at the campground entrance—210 is on his way over there. Do you copy?" So Jason is on his way to the entrance now.

"Ten-four, 223, I read you loud and clear—210 on way to campground entrance, that's good news. Can you come help set up Base Ops in the residential area? We've got between sixty and eighty people en route and we're already out of room here. Tracker One, do you read? Base out."

(*Do I read?* Surely somebody's playing a joke here, but no, it's all quite real. Both Jason and Skip are being called off this tracking team because they're needed elsewhere. From the sound of things, unless there's some mistake, I'm the only tracker here until Riverside arrives.)

"223 to Base, I copy and am on my way in. Hannah's got the track. 223 over and out." No mistake. Walking to my left, I prepare to cut for sign on the far side of the rocky section.

"Tracker One to Base. Any word from Riverside?"

"They're about an hour and fifteen out yet. We'll get them to your location as soon as they arrive. Meantime keep us advised of any changes in direction. We'll have choppers in the air in fifteen minutes and we'll start perimeter cuts on likely roads or trails as soon as we have people to spare out there. Base out."

"Tracker One, copy and out."

0955
Here she is again, finally. Mandy's footprint, still headed away from the campground. I am scared to death right now. It's one thing to practice tracking by yourself—which I've been doing for three months here—and an entirely different thing to be tracking by yourself when a child's life is involved and it's your first real search. Jason was right when he said none of us were

good enough to be doing this. The choppers are in the air. And I think I feel the scent of death in this place.

"Tracker One to Base."

"Go ahead, One."

"Tracks have changed direction and are heading northeast. It'd be good if we could get somebody to cut sign on the old mining road out of the north end of the campground, One out."

"We copy, Tracker One. We'll put the choppers over that area now and get people on it as soon as we have some to spare. Base over and out."

"Headquarters to Search Base."

"Go ahead, HQ."

"Catering truck is on the way with 100 lunches, ETA 0100. Reporter from the local paper should arrive at your location in driving time. HQ over and out."

"Base copy and out." This search is expanding fast.

"Chopper One, Search Base."

"Go ahead, Base."

"Tracker One reports change in track direction. There's an old mining road that leads north out of the top loop of the campground—we'll put somebody out to cut a perimeter on the ground but can you take a look over there for us now? Base out."

"Sure, no problem—Chopper One copies and is outta here."

All right. Dale is in the air. He's the best helicopter pilot around. If anybody can see Mandy from the sky, it'll be him.

1030

Mandy must be following a bunny or a series of bunnies and lizards or lord knows what else that moves: She is wandering all over the place. We've been west and northeast, and now we're heading southwest again. Both choppers have been working back and forth over this area, but no one has seen her yet. The fixed wing hasn't either. I'm still tracking by myself, still scared, but I'm even more afraid of what could happen to Mandy if I bungle my assignment.

The car searches at the park entrances have yielded nothing, which means nothing. If Mandy went to the restroom at 5 A.M., she could've been outside this park by 5:15. Given that her tracks are *here*—and no one else's are as yet—we could stretch that by an hour or so. I'm just hoping and praying, little girl, that you don't wander anywhere near a road: Out here, nobody else is likely to have seen (or threatened) you. A few snakes, a lot of cacti, uneven ground where you might have fallen and sprained an ankle . . . that's it. On the road, we're dealing with an entirely different set of dangers: I'm an adult and quite capable of taking care of myself, yet I wouldn't choose to walk down a road alone in a National Park for anything in this world. You are nine, and two-legged animals are a lot more likely to hurt you than any others, Mandy. So *please* stay out here 'til we can catch up with you, kid! Don't let the scent of death on my shoulder become real again.

Thanks for staying in this wash for a while too—that's a kind thing to do for a green tracker, lets me move a little faster than I could on those rocks.

1105
"Search Base to Tracker One."
    "Go ahead, Base."
    "Riverside's here—we're briefing them now. As soon as we

can get a chopper back here we'll be bringing out two trackers to join you and we'll put the others on perimeter cuts. ID your location for the bird. Base over and out."

"Tracker One copy and out."

ττι5

"Hi there—boy, am I ever glad to see you two!" I say to the two strangers who trot away from the helicopter toward me. Dr. Ed Smith and Jim Calloway, trackers. (They even look like trackers.) I circle one of the better footprints and wait for them.

"What've you got?" Ed asks, pulling out his notebook.

I point to where Mandy's tracks have come from and where they've been heading recently and Jim says, "All right, let's hit it." He motions for me to take point, the lead position.

"Look guys, I think it's time for me to say up front that this is my first search—and I'm sure you two are much better and much faster at this than I am, so if you want me on flank, that's fine, but I'd just as soon one of you take point. We need to find this kid."

Ed looks at me for a second, then says, "Well, from what we've seen so far—from the briefing at the base and here—you're as much a tracker as anybody and that includes us. You've already done half of the work, and we need you on this team, so if you want to flank awhile because you're tired, that's okay, but otherwise stay on point—it'll give us a chance to get to know this kid's tracks."

So that's that. They have more confidence in me than I do in myself. "Tracker One to Search Base—Team One is on the tracks again. One over and out."

"We copy, Team One. Base out." Ed and Jim flank out behind

me on either side, their eyes scanning the ground for any signs that Mandy has changed direction, and I move ahead on her tracks. One step at a time.

1130

Wow! What a difference it makes to have three people working together as a team: We've been racing over the ground like hounds. But just up ahead there's a nasty stretch of rocks, and we're about to lose Mandy for the first time since Ed and Jim got here.

"We need to cover some ground—maybe we ought to start jumping," Ed says.

"Jumping?" I ask, since I'm fairly certain he's not talking literally.

"Yeah," Jim says. "One flanker will fan out left, while the other fans out right—way out, both of them—and then they'll cut for sign while moving forward and back toward each other [and with luck, toward an intersection with the tracks]. Point stays put, step by step, until we get a confirmed track ahead—then we all jump to it—kind of a modified leap frog. It's fast when you have three really good trackers. Shall we?" Although I've never tried it before, the concept makes sense. The flankers will basically cut for sign in two concentric circles forward from the last track, while the point person moves forward from that track as usual. This should speed things up considerably.

"Okay by me, but I want to stick with the step-by-step since that's the only formal training I've had—y'all take off!" I say, grinning but feeling nervous again. "I'll just bring up the rear!"

Ed and Jim disappear to the right and left, and I restart Mandy's track just beyond the rocky section.

1140

Ed calls out, "Jim, come take a look!" Then they both call me, "Hey Hannah, we're somewhere near your ten o'clock!" I circle Mandy's last track and trot toward their voices, looking back occasionally so I can retrace my steps more easily.

"Wow," I say, standing between them looking at Mandy's print. "That's her!"

"All right, let's hit it again, team!" Jim says, and he and Ed disappear once more. For the first time today, I'm beginning to have faith in tracking as a technique. It is working. I start calling Mandy's name every few minutes, as do Jim and Ed. We are going to find this little girl.

1220

We're moving fast. This jump track method is amazing—and fun. But the urgency in our voices as we call for Mandy suggests that we're not enjoying the fun very much. Mandy's tracks are wandering almost erratically now, and the sun's high. Base probably has ten or twelve other trackers out, people on practically every road in this vicinity, but we're the only team to make contact with Mandy's tracks yet, which means we could be very close to finding her. Or very far away.

"Search Base to Tracking Team One."

"Go ahead, Base."

"We've got another tracking team to dispatch. Report current direction of tracks."

"North-northeast. We still need a perimeter cut on that old mining road out of the campground. Team One out."

"Search Base to Chopper Two."

"Go ahead, Base."

"Have a transport from the LZ to the far end of that old mining road, what's your ETA to base?"

"Five minutes, tops. Chopper Two over and out."

"Hey Hannah, we're at your nine o'clock!" I circle Mandy's print and start trotting toward Ed's voice.

"What do you think?" Jim asks me as I crouch down to look at the indistinct print on the ground.

"That's not her," I say slowly, a little uncomfortable to be disagreeing.

"It's not got the detail, maybe, but it's the same size—and we haven't been getting detail for a long time now," Ed says.

"Besides, nobody else would be wandering around out here —we've seen what, maybe ten other people altogether?" Jim adds.

"It's not her, guys. Look how her foot hits the ground here on the outside—Mandy's doesn't do that. This is somebody else." I say, getting surer by the second, looking ahead at the next few indistinct tracks to check my conclusion.

"Are you sure?" Ed asks.

"Positive. Look—even the stride is too long. And it's too old, may have been made several days ago." (To someone who hasn't spent a lot of time in this desert, that set of tracks probably looks like it could've been made this morning, but footprints can be deceptive here.)

"All right then, we'd better cut this one again."

"Well, I'm going back to point," I say.

1245
"Hannah, let's try this again—we're at your two o'clock."

"On my way."

Ed and Jim are crouched down over the track, but they move aside to let me join them.

"That's her again—good job, you guys!" I say, genuinely happy now. "We're going to find this kid yet! *Mandy!* Can you hear us?"

We hit it again, jump tracking for all we're worth.

1345

"Tracking Team Eight to Search Base."

"Go ahead, Eight."

"We've done a sign cut of the old mining road all the way to the campground—she hasn't crossed this yet. Do you copy?"

"Base copy, Tracking Team One do you copy?"

"That's affirmative. Our tracks are heading straight for that road right now and we're within an eighth of a mile of being on it ourselves. We'll keep you advised. Team One out." Then to Ed and Jim, I yell, "Hey, did you hear *that*?!" If Mandy hasn't crossed that road yet—and hasn't doubled back on us—we may be very close to finding her.

Ed and Jim both yell yes, and then we all call out, nearly in unison, "Mandy, can you hear us?"

I'm on point in the middle of a sandy wash which will intersect with that mining road. Come on, Mandy—answer us! *Be here*, little girl!

1400

"Hey Hannah—we're at your nine o'clock!"

Oh no, Mandy, please don't go off in that direction—it's miles to anywhere! For the first time all afternoon I don't trot toward Jim and Ed. I stand still, eyes shut but turned toward the sky.

"Mandy, can you hear me?" I call out hoarsely and then turn to walk toward the guys.

Then all of a sudden, this waif of a girl appears, running down the center of the wash toward me:

"I'm Mandy and my parents have gotten lost!" she calls out.

"Oh really?" I say, dropping to my knees and hugging her close. "Whew, am I ever glad to see you, young lady!"

Mandy insists, "My parents got lost and I can't find them anywhere!"

"They're over at my house, not too far from the campground. We'd better give them a call."

"Tracking Team One to Search Base."

"Go ahead, Team One."

"We've just met a young lady out here named Mandy Evans who's looking for her parents—who've gotten lost—end quote!"

There's a general hurray from a lot of locations in this desert, I know, even though I can hear only those within a quarter mile or so. Ed and Jim are here before I even sign off the radio. Mandy agrees that a helicopter ride would be nice, so she and Ed take the first ride out. Jim and I sit on a rock and wait for our turn. "It's been a good day," I say, "We'd never have found her without you and Ed."

"Sure you would've," Jim says, grinning. "But with only a one-man team, it would have been several hours later!" He's quiet for a few seconds, then adds, "Nobody can jump alone."

1700

Debriefing. We watched videos shot from the helicopters, which had to have flown over Mandy repeatedly, but even Dale never saw her. It's hard to see little things from a chopper.

I'm in the spotlight, thanks to my generous partners, Ed and Jim and Skip, and receiving all kinds of credit for tracking skills that I myself didn't know I had before today. I kept saying, "Well, I'm just really glad to see that all this stuff works in real life," and tried my best to fade into the creosote bushes nearby.

Then Jay Simms, the ranger who heads up Joshua Tree Search and Rescue (JOSAR), came over and dragged me back, saying, "If anybody here should be wearing a yellow JOSAR shirt, it's you—I'll order your shirt myself first thing tomorrow morning!"

And Ed says, "Good—she'll need it when she comes down to help us next time we get called out and need another tracker."

Frank finally asked me to go down to Mandy's campsite and visit with her about what she might do if she ever got lost again. Mandy was in a talkative mood, fully recovered from her fright and proud of having ridden in a real helicopter. Before anyone else was up that morning, she had gone to the restroom and then happened to see a "little bitty rabbit" on her way back to the camper. After following the rabbit for awhile, she saw a "pretty blue and green lizard" and after that she got thirsty and called her parents, "only they didn't answer because they were probably still sleeping."

"And then I couldn't find them anywhere!" Mandy remarked indignantly.

I laughed aloud, and the two of us talked some about what Mandy could do if her parents ever wandered off like that again. A few minutes into the conversation, Mandy looked up suddenly and said sharply, "Do you mean that I was lost, and they weren't?"

"Yes."

"Hmpf," Mandy grunted, scuffing her left foot in the sand. "I didn't feel lost."

"What did you feel?"

There was a long silence, then an answer in a subdued tone. "Scared. I felt really scared."

"Yeah, that's just how I felt the first time I got lost. But there are things you can do to keep that from happening again, you know."

The hour we spent talking about those things was the most satisfying time of the entire debriefing for me. Down time. This was what tracking was all about.

———

I received my bright yellow JOSAR shirt the next week, but not before I'd been confronted by several Park Service employees or SAR team members I only vaguely knew: people who wanted to know why *I* was chosen to be on "the finding team." That I was the only tracker at Cottonwood when Mandy's father showed up for help did not seem to have occurred to any of them, nor did it matter once I mentioned it. Two of these people were out of town when the search happened, and three more had been home but "didn't have the time to come and help" with the search. The term "finding team" was absurd: Everyone on that search—every person in the field or at base—was responsible for finding Mandy. We all had done a good job. I was invited to join the search-and-rescue team because they saw that I had useful skills that day, and I was given the shirt as a sign of my membership. But the shirt was not simply a status symbol. It was important for entirely practical reasons: In the future it would help helicopter pilots and other searchers to see me more easily in the field.

I liked that yellow shirt. It always reminded me of sitting in the dusk talking to Mandy Evans about her lost parents. It meant that I was now officially part of a search-and-rescue team, with a lot of hard work ahead of me. But I did not like the fact that the shirt brought me both resentment and praise. No uniform—no matter how bright a color it is—can create community when jealousy takes hold.

Training with a SAR team meant that I soon had to come to grips with my own eccentricities. One day, after we had rescued a fallen climber before a crowd of tourist cameras, Terry (one of the JOSAR members) passed by me, grinned, and nodding toward our audience's lenses, said, "You gotta love the rush!"

I smiled back to be polite, but thought to myself, "You're talking to the wrong person, man." I did not "love the rush" at all, preferring instead to view what I did as work—hard work, plain and simple. The heroes-out-saving-lives part, what's commonly called the "action junkie" aspect of SAR, seemed to me to fuel a dangerous competitiveness that too easily erupted into the likes of Jason's behavior during the Mandy Evans search. I distrusted that part of my job every bit as much as I enjoyed the hard work. Heroes belong in books and on movie screens. They're a pain in the neck in real life. I don't want to be around them, and I certainly don't want to be one. I can get a more satisfying "rush" from rock climbing.

But Terry's comment raised an important point. In SAR work, a certain tendency toward the "action junkie" mentality is nearly inevitable. In part it arises from being on call twenty-four hours a day and in training every spare minute of the time you're not on a search. When you live with your gear packed so that you can respond within minutes—and stay gone as long as necessary—you learn to enjoy the callouts, the missions that make all the rest of your work worthwhile. The "action junkie" mentality also springs from an honest concern for people's lives: The search-and-rescue motto, "So that others may live," is a strong statement of values. Most searchers care a great deal about human life. Otherwise why would they bother searching for anyone?

Unfortunately, the most negative aspects of this mentality are fostered by the need of outsiders (e.g., journalists) to find "heroes" to stand at the center of compelling stories. Trackers and search-dog handlers are good candidates for these tales, it seems. Something about the work we do lends itself to the "heroic" stereotype, and most of us are too busy working to realize that we need to be dodging reporters or photographers. The fact is that in these cultural tales, individual trackers often get too much credit for successful searches. Trackers seldom if ever work alone, and even when they do so from necessity, they are almost always backed up by a sizable contingent of people doing everything from directing traffic to feeding searchers to dispatching base radio operations. On a search, then, the cook is every bit as crucial to success as any of its trackers.

Media coverage that focuses too much on the tracker simply fuels ugly competitiveness among people who are members of the same team—people who all deserve attention in any stories being constructed. "Hero" stories make key people feel left out and useless while those who are eccentric enough to want to spend hundreds of hours following footprints on the ground are called "heroic" (which does exactly nothing useful for anyone, as far as I can tell). Competition, despite its supposed usefulness elsewhere, is a search team's worst enemy: If you're doing the job to best someone else's effort, you might as well quit and go play hockey—the lost person will probably be better off without your "assistance."

Jason is an extreme example of what can happen when searchers lose sight of what is most important—the lost person's life—or forgot that tracking is an activity that demands teamwork above all else. The employees and volunteers who were annoyed at not having been part of the "finding team" during the Mandy Evans search were motivated by a similar personal competitiveness: Being part of a team is not enough when you are too dependent on the action-junkie routine. *Finding* the lost person isn't enough either; an action junkie is often addicted not just to action, but to the need to seem heroic, outstanding in the field, one eye on the camera.

I've always thought that those who manage to do anything for anyone else—regardless of where they happen to be at the moment of "the find"—are heroic. And as for the notion of "outstanding in the field"? To me that means exactly what it says: "out standing in the field"—sometimes twiddling thumbs like the rest of us and wondering what to do next. The yellow JOSAR shirt was a useful piece of equipment, a practical part of my uniform: I could be seen from the air and the ground. All the kudos for my performance (which might have been textbook-quality, but was far from brilliant) at the debriefing and elsewhere simply created divisions between people who were supposed to work together. One thing I would bet my life on is this: No team divided will ever be able to jump.

The scent of death that rode my shoulder throughout the day as we looked for Mandy had real, if remembered, substance: a lingering taste of the air that had surrounded a homicide victim three weeks earlier. Sunday afternoon. An unidentified male, shot once and left alongside the Old Dale, a dirt road that led to an old mining district, was found by a visitor who'd had the unfortunate luck to take a lunch break near the body. By the time I arrived at the scene, there were sheriff's deputies' footprints everywhere—obliterating all but one partial print of the person who had probably dragged the dead man to the place he was found. With little to do but wait for the coroner to arrive, I sat and stood and paced, trying to ignore the officers' bad jokes and resisting the odor of decay—unsuccessfully, as it turned out, for the smell stayed in my throat and nose and eyes for weeks.

Outside funeral homes, human death has a dry, scorched, musky smell, and an undeniable immediacy. Whatever the chemical composition of that odor, it surely must be species-specific: There wasn't the slightest chance of my mistaking it for the smell of a dead animal. In my lifetime I've been around many of those—dead dogs and cats, horses, cows, birds, snakes. And I've been around a fair number of dead people, too. But before that Sunday, those people were all in coffins, carefully done up to look and smell as inoffensive as possible. In funeral homes, death has the stench of dark red roses—cascades of them spilling over the casket and in standing wreaths lining the walls—enough to make a strong person choke.

But there wasn't a single rose within miles that afternoon, and the stranger lying alongside the Old Dale Road etched a more willful scent of death into my brain: a visceral flash that recurs without warning, and one that doesn't truly go away, no matter how far from the moment I've moved. Give me a warm summer afternoon, sun hanging low in the sky, a turn of the head to the left into the wind and the past? And there it is. A musky reminder of one of the boundaries of my particular species: We too die.

"It was probably a drug deal gone bad," the sheriff's investigator said later, and one of the rangers commented, "You know, drugs may actually be beneficial—at least they help clean out some of the scum." The dead man had black skin and some apparent connections to known narcotics dealers. The last thing I heard about the case was that it was unsolvable and probably not worth solving anyway. There are crimes of all varieties, of course, but the ones we ignore surely say as much about our society's values as those we claim to abhor.

One year after coming to California with a suitcase filled with guns, Kevin called and asked me to pick up the children because he wanted them to live with Frank and me. For weeks we lived on an emotional rollercoaster: One day Kevin would call to say that only Ruthie could come; then the next day he would call and say Jon would be allowed to come too, provided I promised to enroll him in karate; a few days later, he phoned to tell me that Ruthie wasn't going to get to come after all because she was "already too much like her mother anyway," but Jon could still come if I agreed to buy him a new four-wheeler within seven days of his arrival. In the end, Kevin only let Ruthie come to live with Frank and me.

Older now, one of the first things Ruthie asked me was "Why do they let Daddy hurt us, Mom?" There was no anger in her eyes, just a single question, calmly put. My daughter was slowly comprehending the societal values in which we were all trapped. She was also learning to put one foot in front of the other.

Suicide, too, is a crime, and it's one that the National Park Service takes fairly seriously. But there is no kind of search that drains me more and makes me wonder why on earth I ever took up tracking.

It's not that I'm queasy or unnerved about walking into a potentially gruesome scene. Nor am I afraid, although some people intent on committing suicide have been known to be rather unfriendly to anyone who tries to stop them. And I certainly have no moral baggage about the ethics of choosing to end one's life. To be honest, although I had not considered it as a way out for myself in 1987, I'd always thought rather abstractly that suicide was probably the only rational response to an irrational world. Why it was against the law mystified me, so getting called out on the Eldon Keith search in Joshua Tree was initially annoying more than anything else. After taking Ruthie to Al and Rita's trailer, Frank and I packed our gear to head to the north side of the Monument, with me grumbling to myself and openly wishing they'd find the guy before we even got there.

As we reached the staging area and I was snapping on Sam's leash, I heard one of the rangers say, "We've got a note from inside Keith's truck."

In an aside to Frank, I said darkly, "The guy's probably sitting up there in the rocks smoking a cigarette and enjoying the sunshine and laughing at us poor fools."

Frank frowned at my tone and joined the others. I lagged behind with Sam, then finally walked over to look at the sheet of paper everyone else was inspecting. It was a rumpled piece of notebook paper that looked like a schoolchild's punishment: From top to bottom were handwritten lines, all saying exactly the same thing.

I, Eldon Keith, do forgive myself, no matter what.
I, Eldon Keith, do forgive myself, no matter what.
I, Eldon Keith, do forgive myself, no matter what.
I, Eldon Keith, do forgive myself, no matter what.
I, Eldon Keith, do forgive myself, no matter what.
I, Eldon Keith, do forgive myself, no matter what.
I, Eldon Keith, do forgive myself, no matter what.
I, Eldon Keith, do forgive myself, no matter what.
I, Eldon Keith, do forgive myself, no matter what.

The last few lines were smudged and less even than the rest, and the final one trailed off with no punctuation.

The smell of death was back on my shoulder, this time accompanied by a leaden sensation at the back of my throat. Eldon was not going to be alive when we found him. I had an urgent desire to rush off, to take Sam and get as far away from this repulsive place as possible. The team would find Eldon, and I didn't want to be there when they did.

Had Frank not called me right then, I might well have walked off. But they'd found a glove in Eldon's truck and thought we might be able to use it as a scent article. Turning a plastic bag inside out, I picked up the glove without touching it. Great scent article at least, I thought to myself. The best ones are pieces of clothing that have been worn next to the body and haven't been handled by other people. Sam examined the glove and then sat waiting beside me while we got our assignment. Short-handed, we'd be going out in teams of two for the time being. The best guess was that Eldon, whose truck was left parked at a motel in Twentynine Palms, had walked south into the Monument.

Sam and Martin (a newer JOSAR member) and I were sent to

cut a perimeter along the base of the hills that run east and west inside the Monument's northern boundary. We had no idea what kind of shoes Eldon might have been wearing. For that matter, note notwithstanding, we had no real information that he might have decided to kill himself. But he had been missing for several days, he was depressed when he left home, and we had found a sheet of paper that at the very least didn't sound as if Eldon had happily embarked on an impromptu camping trip.

As Martin and I trudged along over the rocks with Sam air-scenting ahead, I retreated into the dark humor that had often so puzzled me when I'd observed it in law enforcement rangers. "All right Marty, when we come across this guy, here's the deal— *you* are elected to go through his pockets, you hear me? I'm from the South and we don't believe in dealing with corpses unless they're in caskets!"

Marty looked at me and grinned. "No way, partner! This is a fifty-fifty team straight up the center. You'll take one pocket, I'll take the other—that way nobody gets a headstart if he sits up all of a sudden."

A few hours of sign-cutting (and sick humor) later, we checked in at the base, our quadrant covered and nothing to report. Frank and Sam headed off in a helicopter to the top of the hills to check out a prominent drainage, and I took a stint dispatching. The search was proceeding smoothly, and talk around the base kept returning to the possibility that Eldon had just skipped out on his girlfriend (an all-too-common occurrence in missing person cases). The search boss called all the teams in for the night, with plans to start again at daybreak, and I went to sleep, wishing I was home to tuck Ruthie into bed, telling myself that this Eldon Keith character must be hula-dancing the night away with some lady friend in Hawaii.

The next morning we crawled out of our sleeping bags to listen to the plan for the day: The helicopter would be depositing us in teams of two at various locations along the hills and we'd systematically rule out all the drainage systems by a series of perimeter cuts. The first team climbed aboard the chopper while the rest of us sorted out the most efficient order for the pilot to transport us in. Suddenly, not sixty seconds after taking off, the chopper made a wide circle and started back toward us, preparing to land about a city block west from where we were standing. Six or seven of us said almost in unison, "They've got him."

It was over. I picked up my search pack—no more need for it—and walked to the truck. Sure enough, the radio in my chest harness crackled with the inevitable words: "We have an 1144." Eldon Keith was dead. Had been for nine days. He'd taken a shotgun and blown his brains out. Damn. For the last ten hours or so I'd been trying to picture the man on a sneak trip to the islands. To make a bad moment much worse, the search boss looked over at me and suggested that I go and talk to Eldon's sister, who was waiting anxiously near her car. Eileen wasn't surprised, but she began quietly crying. I had no details to give her, so could only stand there like a stump in my bright yellow shirt, trying to offer some comfort in a situation where nothing at all was going to help.

"What will I tell my daughter? She's crazy about her Uncle Eldon!" Eileen sobbed, and I felt even more like a yellow stump until Frank asked me to come help him with something. By then there were several less stumplike people standing with Eileen, so I mumbled a few words and left.

Practical to the core, Frank suggested that we take Sam over to the body because he'd never actually been around "a ripe one" before (the situation was sometimes a hard one to come by in dog training), so we did just that. Until the moment I looked down at Eldon Keith's body decomposing there on the desert sand, suicide had been a theoretical concept. A perfectly rational response to an irrational world. But when I reached Eldon, the concept became terrifyingly real—and all I wanted to do was stand him up and shake a knot in him. Blindingly angry at this stranger for being so selfish as to leave a sister and niece and girlfriend behind to worry and wonder and to hurt for the rest of their lives—well, damn him! I stalked off toward the west, leaving Sam with Frank, intending to take a very long, roundabout route back to base. Sam caught up with me a few minutes later, seeming none the worse for his encounter with a corpse, and we walked along together. How dare one person put so many other people out? The hours we'd all spent banging around on the rocks the day before? And all the time the jerk was lying there *dead*?

On the way back into base I crossed a set of tracks headed for the Monument. Pretty certain they were Eldon's, I stopped. Sure enough, the treads matched the shoes on his feet (his shoes were probably the first thing I looked at when we reached his body— after all, it was his feet or his face, and the feet were closer to me and infinitely less disturbing). With Sam close beside me, I sat down and looked at those tracks. Determined. Perhaps slow and measured, but definitely determined. No hint of hesitation. I took a long pause to rethink the man I thought I knew minutes before. No hint of selfishness. No signs of a jerk in the vicinity. Simply the footprints of a man who had just written over and over, "I, Eldon Keith, do forgive myself, no matter what." A man who then took his shotgun, locked his truck, and headed south.

What despair could have made Eldon leave these tracks? The

scent of death had left my shoulder and was in the air all about, mingling with the smell of creosote bushes, rustling with palpable reality through the dry arms of a desert birdcage near one of Eldon's footprints. Sam and I soon headed for the truck.

The afternoon air was still as Frank and I drove home, saying little. This had not been a rewarding experience, and neither of us had the heart to pretend it had been. Ruthie welcomed us with a smile and a handful of garden flowers, but sleep was still long in coming that night and for many that followed it. Eldon Keith's footprints had touched a woman on the verge of serious withdrawal. From that moment, although I didn't know it then, I was on my way out of the Park Service and back into my life.

The next day's paper had a large front-page photo of me examining Eldon's glove (where that photographer came from I'll never know). Once again I had been singled out for attention—as in the Mandy Evans search—and for an even less memorable contribution to "the find." Non-trackers to a person, most of them not trained to work in the field and not one of them who knew one thing about me beyond my name and my face, a few jealous people openly criticized me and those attached to me, including Frank. I responded by backing away from everyone: leaving training sessions early or not going at all; avoiding the drinking parties; wandering off into the desert, tracking nothing in particular; responding to search calls but trying to melt into the crowd on arrival at any search base.

The adversarial atmosphere persisted, and when one day another JOSAR team member refused to communicate the status of a search by radio to Frank, who was Acting Chief Ranger for the Monument that weekend, I turned in my bright yellow shirt and began a determined walk toward a world where people didn't compete with everything that moves. Looking not just for colleagues, but for a society that wouldn't give you more credit than you ought to have, wouldn't create false heroes in situations where everyone qualified or no one did, wouldn't perpetuate the myth that competition is more productive than cooperation, wouldn't abandon children to a father's anger—or women to a man's—simply because of a biological or legal tie.

College seemed the most logical destination. Anthropology, a discipline based on attempts to understand human societies, might have some answers. But first I headed home to the South, trying to reconnect with some of the more hopeful parts of myself. To find once more, if possible, the girl who lived in and was thankful for—but did not worship or need to master—the natural environment.

The evening primrose has creamy white, translucent blossoms: as near perfect as flowers get and delicate as gossamer. The blooms stand on slender stems that lean their heads toward one another as the plant dries; when their swaying ceases at the end of the season, when the flowers have long since ceased to reflect the morning sun, the plant transforms itself into a gently rounded birdcage. Sand settles on the bottom, anchoring the cage to the ground. Leaves blow past, spiders spin silky webs about the dry stems and lizards scuttle through, people walk by and leave their footprints on the ground. Step by step.

Every time I see an evening primrose, I remember sitting there with Sam on the ground next to Eldon Keith's footprints, listening to the soft wind rattle through the desert birdcage, passing us all. But now I also remember taking Ruthie to find her first evening primrose; I see again the many trips we made that spring and summer, watching the plant transform itself into the dried cage that so delighted my daughter. I remember how our footprints wore a path through the desert from the house to that primrose. And I will never forget the look on my childrens' faces when Jon finally came to live with us and his sister took him to see *her* birdcage—which she proudly presented with its hyphenated, "but still pretty," name: the "thera-delty primrose." *Oenothera deltoides*, evening primrose.

MARKING THE TRACK

WHEN A TRACKER finally finds the footprint that may be that of the person she's looking for, she doesn't rush off on the trail immediately—that kind of behavior is best saved for the movies. In the real world, even when you're working alone, it is likely that someone else may come along and need to know what set of prints you are following. When you are part of a team, then, you must behave as if the information you're carrying around in your head will be needed by someone else later. So you mark the track: by drawing a circle around it on the ground and tying a piece of bright-colored flagging to the nearest bush. You communicate your location to search base as well, and only then are you free to move out on the tracks.

Ten hours later, when the size of the search has quadrupled and you're two miles from that marked track, a team from two states away can not only arrive, find your marked track, and be briefed on where it went from there, but can then be flown to a new area to start cutting another perimeter for that footprint. Marking the track, then, as pedestrian as it may seem, stands at the very center of competent search tactics.

The place of my youth, rural southern Mississippi, operated by a set of rules that I understood even when I disagreed with them. Simple rules about people—children, especially, and how they're supposed to behave themselves. Things like respecting your elders; saying Ma'am and Sir; doing your chores without having to be told; not bragging or thinking highly of yourself; doing everything to the best of your ability, but carefully avoiding competing with others (after all, you might actually win and hurt their feelings); and avoiding anger or violence—even harsh words—assiduously.

Possessing no natural talent for religion, I wound up taking my parents' evangelical Christianity, which was both strict and internally inconsistent, as many religions are, and made up my own version of the rules. Never entirely sure that our preachers were wrong about the existence of hell, I chose a safe, middle-of-the-road approach to God and built my life at least partially on Jesus' teachings—the "blesseds," especially. One of them I liked better than all the rest: "Blessed are the meek, for they shall inherit the earth." Now *that* was a sentence worth living by—especially for a youngster who preferred the woods to any house any day. Outside was where I belonged.

⸻

Although no one in my childhood ever suggested that "tracking" was a distinctive activity, had someone pointed it out as such and defined it, I would've instantly said that tracking was hunting, and hunting was a man's job. I would also have said that only men tracked and hunted. But that would not have been entirely true.

While only men hunted, women like my grandmother and children like me paid careful attention to signs on the ground— we "tracked" the presence and meaning of those signs on a daily basis. But, unlike the men, we didn't usually *talk* about tracking. My father and his friends, on the other hand, talked animal tracks instead of sports, and any one of them could not only identify an animal just by looking at its spoor, but also tell you what that animal did, where it went and when, and sometimes why and how fast. Clearly these were things only men could find fascinating, I thought, and I spent the first few years of my life avoiding these male conversations religiously.

Hunting was a reality of my youth that I never learned to appreciate or understand. I disliked everything associated with it—the guns, bullets, game bags, camouflage clothing, and noise—wishing fervently that we had enough money so hunting wasn't a necessity. But I also begged my father to take me coon hunting from the time I was old enough to figure out that hunting allowed him to be in the woods several hours a night while I was stuck in the house—until he finally relented and took me. Long before we returned home that morning, I'd decided I would much prefer being stuck in the house to chasing down and killing animals, and I never again asked to go.

Paying attention to signs on the ground, following them only out of curiosity, then, I was not technically a tracker. Had I been asked about any youthful interest in tracking, I would have denied it point blank and not been lying. But the day I discovered a pragmatic use for the skill, all that began to change.

The hunting seasons of my seventh and eighth years I had spent in the woods actively subverting the hunters. During the rest of the year I walked quietly in an attempt to blend in with my surroundings, but throughout hunting season I crashed loudly about on either my horse or my own two feet, clapping my hands and screeching or banging a spoon on a tin can, hoping that all animals within hearing range would assume a lunatic had entered the woods and leave for their own safety and sanity. One day after overhearing the men talking, I realized that tracking could help me warn the animals more efficiently—if I could recognize the animals' tracks quickly, it seemed I'd stand a better chance of scaring more of them off than I did by just trooping through the woods noisily. I began to pay very close attention to what my father said about following animals and quickly learned that by combining what the men said about tracking with close observation of what they looked at in the woods or along the gravel roadsides, I could begin to piece together some of the basics for myself. Eavesdropping on the men's hunting conversations became my first order of business.

Those men could talk for two hours straight about one raccoon that had a unique right front pawprint or a deer that had a slightly turned left back hoof. In five minutes I always felt the topic should have been exhausted and was ready for a turn in the conversation, but they would keep on talking. Most remarkable was the way the men seemed to want to learn everything possible about animal habits and haunts, about plants, weather, soils, and streams. These men knew how raccoons normally crossed Muddy Springs Creek near the bend south of Ed Hillenbrand's place, so when one grizzled fellow unexpectedly took a new route one night, his every step was recounted in detail. By the time the men finished talking, I was usually pretty sure that they had broken some deep law of nature about getting too close. Basically I wanted (and truth tell, still want) the mysteries of the woods to remain, not to be pinned to a wall and dissected with words and laughter and hunting plans. So I kept quiet, trying to learn to follow by listening.

The basics came together quickly in my head. The real challenge would be to see if I could actually follow an animal somewhere and find that same animal at the end. So, to test my accuracy, I worked backward: I found an occupied rabbit hole, sat down a long way from it until the rabbit came out, and then watched and memorized the rabbit's route. Invariably, if I jumped up at just the right time, the rabbit would head back to the hole—leaving me with a whole round trip of tracks to follow. That is not the smartest or most efficient way to learn to track, and the rabbits could not have enjoyed it much, but it was a start.

Over time I got more confident of my eyes and began to trust what they saw on the ground. And while tracking did help me find the animals, it was entirely peripheral to my work. If I lost a track, no problem, I'd just set in to yelling or banging a pan with my spoon sooner than I might have had to otherwise (demented behavior to which no hunter in his right mind would ever resort). The men would have been appalled.

Tracking marked the edges of one of the unspoken lines in southern society: men were on one side of the line; women were on the other. Men hunted; women did not. And while we may not have spoken about that line aloud, not a one of us would have denied its existence, at least not to a close friend. Opposed it? Yes, in a silent, undirected sort of way. Sabotaged it? Certainly, repeatedly, with varying degrees of success. Dispensed with it entirely, given the opportunity? Probably not.

Anyway, a line that seems so fixed in one situation may disappear completely in another. Tracking did not belong exclusively to southern men. Women like my Mammaw Ruth also paid attention to signs on the ground, and I never doubted that, had she ever needed to, my grandmother could have hunted as well as any man. The killing part wouldn't have bothered her like it did other women either, mostly because Mammaw didn't see any difference between killing a wild animal (like a deer or squirrel) and a domesticated one (such as a pig or steer). "As long as people have to eat, young'un," she'd say, "somebody's got to do the dirty work." And then she would roll up her sleeves and get on with it.

My mother's mother was Ruth Haney; we called her Mammaw Ruth whenever she wasn't around and Mammaw Haney whenever she was. Tall and dark-skinned, with a strong nose and cheekbones and large hands with long fingers, Mammaw wore her name as if it were written in neon lights on a three-story marquee. "Ruth's a strong name, meant for a strong woman—and you won't find a woman nor man alive what's stronger than *this one*," she used to say, pointing one of those long fingers at herself emphatically and sniffing haughtily at the same time. I, of course, never doubted her for a second.

Mammaw Ruth was a Sioux Indian—at least that's what she always said, and until I was eight I was much too scared of her to doubt her word on *anything*, much less her tribal identity. Actually, what was most noticeable and memorable about my grandmother was the plain fact that she was one *mean* woman. And by that I do not suggest that she was a "ladylike mean," as are many southern women, for she was nothing of the sort: Ruth Haney's hands were not "gentle but firm"—they were tough as sturdy oak bark and most everything she did with them was convincing. Not many people crossed her and got away with it. Of course, if I'd had to live her life—poor, not-white, from 1899 through the 1960s in southern Mississippi—I probably would be harder to cross than I currently am, too.

Some people never leave you. Mammaw Ruth is one of those. Her sayings still ground my world: haughty, proudly tossed words like, "Ain't sleepin with 'em—wouldn't like to be" (which meant she couldn't care less what they thought of her). So do odd moments that crystallize instantaneously at the sound of an irritable car horn in traffic. Mammaw, snuff container in her right hand, yanking the steering wheel of her old Ford truck (and us) around to the left and tossing that snuff container into the ash tray at the same time, snorting with disgust as someone from behind honked their horn to protest her cutting in front of them. Me looking back to check—sure enough, it was a pale, weak-looking white woman—and Mammaw yelling at the top of her lungs, "*Blow it—You sure can't suck it, honey!*" Throwing her head back and laughing at her own joke, which I, predictably, didn't get. Catching my eye, grinning widely and telling me, "Don't you ever let 'em push you around, gal." Then she'd lay her left hand on the horn, gun the engine, yank the wheel back straight, and we'd be long gone.

Memories that challenge my certainties: How can tracking be a male thing when every time we went outside, Mammaw Ruth would "read the trees and the ground," saying things like "Those deer were back in here again last night," pointing to their tracks in the dirt and to the places where they'd nibbled at her peas? How can fear of reptiles be encoded in maternal genetics if Mammaw Ruth could walk along her lily beds, pick off two little green lizards, and attach one to each ear lobe—the lizards would chomp down onto her ears and then wouldn't let go, they'd just hang there, tails dangling like a long, fancy pair of ear bobs as Mama and I screamed and ran away with Mammaw grinning and chasing us, hollering things like, "Aw, come on back here—y'all are worse cowards than them Choctaw what we keep on the reservation up north!" And there's the color question again: How could Mammaw hate the Choctaw people so? I never really asked her out loud, but she answered a few of my quizzical looks with phrases that explained nothing at all to me: "Sell-outs, that's what the whole lot of 'em are." Or "They gave up, but *my people* never quit fighting." Mammaw's explanations could be as bewildering as her actions. And they almost always hurt.

Because as much as I loved my grandmother and wanted to be like her, there was no chance at all that I would ever walk in her shoes, something Mammaw Ruth repeatedly pointed out to me. For I was born with my father's coloring and features: towheaded and fair-skinned with a short, stubby nose and green eyes, traits that annoyed Mammaw no end and elicited some of her harshest comments. Things like "You got that white skin of your daddy's, gal, so you might as well *expect* to be no-count." Or, when I was in serious trouble, some version of "Yep, with that pale skin, I'll leave some blisters you won't be forgettin' soon." But the fact that she didn't seem to like me very much never stopped Mammaw Ruth from telling me her Indian stories, and from them and my books I learned how to behave myself in the woods and the world around me.

After reading a book about how Indians could walk through the woods in all seasons without making a sound, I began trying to acquire that skill—and gave up after two weeks, on deciding that Indians must never have tried to walk through the Mississippi woods in October. When I told Mammaw Ruth about it, she frowned at me and said, "Should've asked me first—I could've told you you ain't never gonna learn anything worth knowing about Indians from the white man's books, young'un." But books were irresistible to me, and a few days later, I had my nose back in another one.

When I read that Indian braves tracked game through the densest brush without losing the trail and then thanked the animal before killing it, I pestered Mammaw into talking to me about hunting and asked if she thought it would be okay for a girl to learn on her own since there weren't any Indian boys around to teach me. Preoccupied with her work, Mammaw just shook her head and said, "Reckon there ain't no harm in it as long as you plan on eatin' whatever you kill."

Successful on the first afternoon, not because I could follow tracks, but because I knew where the rabbit's burrow was, I lay flat on the ground and peered into the hole, close enough to see the tiny toes on the babies, and solemnly thanked that Mama

Rabbit—and then quickly apologized for saying thanks since I wasn't about to whack her over the head with the stick I had commandeered for a spear, and I didn't want the rabbit thinking that was really my intention. I went home that evening half annoyed at having learned that living like A Real Indian meant that I'd have starved if it weren't for my father, who always killed the animals we ate, and half glad that I lived on a farm where the animals we intended to eat were earmarked long before we ever had a chance to get attached to them. Daddy would say of a new calf, "That one'll make good eatin' one day," as good as hanging a billboard around the calf's neck that read, "Do not even consider making friends with this one." Mammaw Ruth never asked how the tracking went, and I never brought it up again. Books and stories don't always mix well.

My feelings for my grandmother go well beyond the warmth I muster for the few people other than my children I'm close to. They're far more fierce, springing as they do from a blinding desire to be even a little bit like her: courageous, robust, and proud, in Ruth Haney's words, "with a backbone of steel and a heart to match"—that is, until the cancer came and ate all the way through Mammaw's spine. Then one day she looked up from her bed and said to me, "Young'un, the steel's all gone now. You'll have to find your own somewhere else."

As Mama took care of Mammaw Ruth through those last two, long months, I sat curled up on the front porch underneath Mammaw's bedroom window, vowing that one day I would be like the woman who was dying a few feet away from me. Unstinting with criticism, so that the tiniest smile conveyed genuine praise, quick to frown but even quicker to laugh. Hardened by life, yet still living it with enthusiasm, right down to the last breath. Having the courage to be angry at a rotten deal, to shout in the face of pain, to rail against something as relentless as the cancer that was killing her, yet still able to tell a meandering story that could fill up a child's whole world. Taking the time to walk that pale little granddaughter down to the spring in the woods, cupping those wrinkled brown hands so she could drink the cold, sweet water. Sitting down with that "bookish" child on the riverbank and telling her where waterbugs came from and why they learned to dance—and that the stories in her science books were probably all lies written by white men somewhere. Walking alongside the tracks of a mad dog that had staggered onto the farm, carrying a double-barreled shotgun slung over her shoulder, wearing a flour-streaked apron, telling the child at her side not to get in the way when the dog was sighted—"otherwise I'll have to shoot you first, and that'd be a waste of a good bullet," then throwing her head back and laughing so loud and hard that her whole body shook and tears streamed down her face. I'd be willing to bet that no men ever had so much fun tracking anything as we did that day.

But maybe that's not quite right. Every year of my life from age one to thirteen, on a day in early spring my father and I would wander along the pasture fences and into the woods looking for violets and the little flowers we called daisies to make a posey for my mother. Barely a quarter-inch across, the four-petaled, faint purple "daisies" always signaled the start of spring at the edge of the yard or fields. The violets grew deeper in the woods, near mossy tree trunks or along the creek banks, and together the two flowers first filled my pockets and later, when I got old enough to realize that flowers should have proper containers, a tiny vase saved especially for the occasion.

Since we couldn't take too many flowers from one place, we'd sometimes tramp about the woods for hours on end. Dark green canopy overhead, rustling pines, and always, the creek splashing quietly alongside the deer trails that served as our paths, paths invisible to strangers. I didn't have any concept of "nature" back then, nor do I remember us ever sitting down to puzzle one out. Nature was simply the woods—and we were often in them.

I always knew that my father didn't go just for the violets, and it was fairly obvious that though we went looking for the same things—animal tracks—we did it for different reasons. He looked at them to understand them better so he could hunt them more successfully when the season opened. That was part of his job. Shoving that information way to the back of my mind, I walked right alongside him and looked at those same tracks so I too could recognize them quicker when hunting season came around—doing *my* job. Fully intending to make his work as a hunter more difficult.

Daddy always said, "We never kill anything we're not going to eat, Sis," like that was supposed to make me feel better, but it didn't—especially when I watched him leave with Mr. Don and their coondogs every night at sunset. They were going to hunt raccoons, animals that I liked better than most people, and I had to watch them leave, saying nothing, and then try to forget these huge differences in the silence of sleep.

If it hadn't been for those violets and daisies, and the patterning of our lives on similar traditions that reminded us we were a family no matter how much we disagreed on things like hunting, my childhood would have been considerably less safe and cheerful.

Spaces in the South are deeply gendered in ways that might surprise outsiders. The house, yard, and vegetable garden were my mother's domain—and the barn, fields, pastures, and woods were my father's. Perhaps contrarily I did everything in my power as a child to get out of the house/yard/garden—with its "women's work"—and into the barn/fields/pastures/woods— where the work was much harder and much more rewarding. For the first thirteen years of my life, my parents were remarkably cheerful about letting their oldest daughter be a tomboy. The fact is, they needed a boy on the farm then much worse than they needed a girl, a small detail I noticed early on and made a point of thanking God for regularly. The woods became my stomping grounds, the place I went whenever farmwork was finished, largely because being there meant that I could usually avoid whatever housework was underway.

Mississippi's woods insisted on one thing above all else: attentiveness. I could be as clumsy and distracted as I liked in the house, the gardens, yard, or fields—but in the woods I had to pay attention. Trailing animals quietly, observing their behavior as well as the sounds they make or the signs they leave on the ground, is a good way to begin developing attention skills. After hundreds of hours in the woods, an attentive person begins to see and hear and smell without actively relying on their eyes or ears or nose. The heightened perceptions that come with repeated trips to the woods eventually allow you to feel the presence of other animals before ever seeing them, to know, for example, that a snake is lying perfectly still ten feet to the left of the trail without having to so much as glance in the snake's direction. Failure to pay attention in the woods, on the other hand, can mean that you have stepped on the snake before you've even seen it. Or gotten lost in a place you ought to know as well as your own backyard.

I remember almost nothing about the hours that preceded the moment I first got lost in our woods. I was probably playing as usual at being an Indian or a pioneer, collecting building materials for my latest project (an unsteady tepee or log cabin or smokehouse or creek dam) and dragging them back to the "homeplace." But this day was different. One moment I was meandering along, no doubt looking closely at the ground, and the next I was staring straight at a tree trunk that I had never seen before in all my life.

No one had ever suggested to me that there might be a technique for getting un·lost, nor did I stand around reflecting on that possibility. I simply did what came naturally: turned my back on that tree and took off running as fast as I could. That didn't last long, because every tree I passed was just as strange as the first one, and it quickly dawned on me that I was only running myself further lost. Winded, I crawled onto a downed trunk and pulled my knees up to my chest and sat there looking around at all those foreign trees.

Praying didn't work. The woods still looked completely unfamiliar. Closing my eyes tight and then slowly reopening them ten times didn't help either. Chin on my knees, I stared around me, afraid of the woods for the first time in my life, hearing strange rustling noises, wishing I could just remember where our house was or that I hadn't sneaked away from it without telling anyone where I was going. Nobody would ever find me here.

Eventually my eyes landed on the ground. There were my tracks—or rather, my marks in the deep leaf groundcover. With each running step I'd kicked up leaves and thus left a clear trail. Hopping off the tree trunk, I started following my tracks back through the woods to that first strange tree. This would work. It *had* to.

It did. Slowly I tracked myself back along the way I'd come earlier, and by dark I had reached trees that I knew well. Soon the lights of our house beckoned through the brush, and I scrambled over the fence into our east pasture feeling a little like I'd just been forced to visit a cemetery. Cold and unnerved. Mammaw Ruth would've called me "witless" if she'd known about the incident. (So I never mentioned it to her.)

Is there ever a way to cut for sign along an old trail without your eyes and mind cleaning it up some? Straightening out the threads of the story, smoothing and arranging them for those who haven't yet heard the tale? Perhaps, in some ways at least, weaving a less tangled pattern for yourself?

I have an uneasy relationship with memories, a vexed alliance with the past. Almost invariably I want to "clean it up," to excise the sad sections and leave out the parts of the story that still hurt, and in the retelling to somehow sidestep those times that, deep down, I cannot forget. If we would only tell and remember the good times, I used to think, perhaps we could draw more of them to ourselves?

"Cleaning things up" is a habit you learn early, before you

have a chance to ponder the extent to which it will constrain your life. It's all well and good to clean things, but when we turn to tidying up the past, whitewashing the events and people who have profoundly shaped us—all of them—we've laid our hands roughly on something priceless: the knowledge that we can walk through pleasure or pain, joy or sadness, with equal grace or clumsiness, as the case may be, that what counts is that we get through somehow. More troubling, perhaps, we've compromised the chance to walk beside the person we follow. The process of walking alongside must account for good and bad alike. Following only the good means we follow a phantom, nothing more. To find the real person, we have to be careful what we clean.

⁂

My mother's memories of Mammaw Ruth span many more years than mine and hold more dark places in which lurk the kind of things that southerners—with the possible exception of the William Faulkner types—prefer to keep quiet about. Things I refused to let my mother tell me until recently, things about her mother that I could not, would not, hear as a child or a teenager or a young adult and that I accept now only reluctantly, even though I know that these were precisely the things that created the woman I love so fiercely. Things like Mammaw Haney's beating her own kids with a stick of firewood or rushing out of the house holding a gun to her head, threatening to kill herself— prevented only by the tearful intervention of her fifteen-year-old daughter, my mother.

Child abuse and depression were not household words during the 1960s, nor in fact are these terms entirely appropriate for my grandmother's world, but the deep sadness of her life was a reality I not only recognized but instinctively withdrew from whenever my mother suggested that my memory was fairly selective concerning Mammaw Ruth. That's not exactly true. I vividly remember doing some yelling of my own, dragging my feet on the floor and pulling against my grandmother's strong hands, as she hauled me toward her bathroom for punishment. Then my own mother's hands and voice intervening, pulling me away from Mammaw and the discipline she intended, and hurrying me out of the house with Mammaw's angry words still ringing in my ears. It wasn't that I didn't know Mammaw Ruth could be cruel, for of course I did. It was more that I preferred not to know it (which required behaving as if I didn't). And anyway, fierce love always reasons, if she behaves like that she probably has very good grounds for doing so. If you really love somebody you have to love them right through the bad times too. So it hurts sometimes? Well, that's life.

Despite my lifelong preference for the outdoors, home has always been one of my most treasured places, thanks to my parents and all those family traditions they gave me. But since my marriage to Kevin, "home" has also been one of my worst nightmares. For while home stands for many of the wonderful human possibilities that exist—security, love, support, family—it also measures with equal force the opposites of "wonderful": fear, loathing, insecurity, a terrifying aloneness, enforced connections with people who don't even like—much less love—you.

My parents' home was not a place of terror—far from it. Fears there were largely residual and fairly benign—heights and snakes, both of which occasioned as much laughter in our family as anything else. Difference was tolerated with reasonable good cheer. The oldest daughter, after all, was not just a tomboy, but oddly antisocial, a voracious reader who had only raccoons and horses as friends. Church was sixty miles away, thus intruding only on Sundays and during occasional camp meetings and revivals. At first, that is. By the time I was twelve, church was still technically sixty miles away, but it had suffused every aspect of daily life. Three years later, religion had fully overtaken—and nearly destroyed—my childhood home. Two years after that, my father and I were not speaking to one another when I married into that church, moved seven hundred miles away from Mississippi, and become a personal punching bag for one of its respected members. God and I got closely acquainted there for a while.

At thirteen, I unwillingly began the move out of childhood. The transition was hard on everyone. Every human in my world was dead set on turning me into a Young Lady—a white one at that—despite the fact that it meant fitting a very large square peg into a tiny round hole. Horseshoeing was out; cooking and sewing were in. Disappearing into the woods was no longer an option; it was time for me to learn "homemaking." I rapidly went from being an outside free spirit to an inside drudge, or at least that's how I saw it. My raccoons—Eddy, Eunice, and Frosty—didn't seem to mind my changed status: they patiently sat in front of the mirror in my room helping me plaster some order into my unruly hair, cheerfully eating my grouchy excuses for cookies, and silently watching with wide eyes when I cried with frustration over a seam that refused to lie flat.

To my way of thinking then, I lost everything. My horse was sold one summer while I was (unhappily) away at camp meetings, and all my raccoons died within a few months of each other. Piano lessons and recitals, which I had enjoyed since third grade, were canceled for good one Sunday when I refused to sing an unplanned solo at the pastor's request during the morning service. My books, probably my most valuable possessions, were deemed by the church as having been responsible for corrupting me, so Mark Twain was out; *The Pilgrim's Progress* was in. Horrified at the turn for the worst my life had taken, I balked mostly in silence until I turned sixteen. Soon afterward, with the hope of love and marriage and a home of my own on my horizons, I relented. Repented too, no less. Became the best practicing Christian I'd ever been (or ever will be again).

And a proper Young Lady too. A little rough around the edges no doubt. Permanently antisocial for one thing. Painfully shy around people. Submissive to the point of having practically no personality at all. Connected to nothing and no one except fragments of childhood dreams that were no longer tangible. Living more than ever in a century before my own, longing to have lived in a world where God liked all his people, not just his Saints, and where everyone had an equal chance at life. The more estranged I became from my parents, the more my dreams beckoned. Dreams of my self: riding a horse out on the prairies; homesteading at a bend in the creek; living in a place and time where my long dresses were no longer connected to religion, so no one laughed at me for wearing them; walking softly through the woods gathering berries or poke leaves; rocking my babies to sleep with Mamma Ruth's stories whispering about their heads; having a partner—one person in the whole world who really loved *me*—and a home with a fireplace and garden. Then Kevin came along, writing poetry, and the dream was tangible.

Dreams may be lovely. But when they're not sorted out in everyday life, they may also be malevolent. Untested, they blind us to things we really ought to be paying attention to so that our spirits are broken long before we realize they were ever being attacked. They erect huge barriers between us and the people we need most, the ones who demonstrated love in the past but no longer know how to reach us. They hide from us the loveliest parts of ourselves and others. Worst of all, they lay a false trail, which we too quickly follow. Into darkness from which there is no retreat without surrendering those dreams—but letting go of them is too hard. So the darkness fades to steely gray. And the dreams start to slip away. (They'll wait this out in a friendlier clime, just in case you don't survive.)

You are now entirely alone. Lost. Too hurt to cry or call out for help. And far too exhausted to track your way back home again.

My parents never dreamed that a man would one day beat me regularly—they'd have been a little less intent on coaxing submissive adolescent behavior from me if they had. Had they realized how forcing me to become a Young Lady would contribute to my acquiescence to a brutal husband, I am certain they would never have let me get anywhere near the kitchen or the sewing machine. Had they known how ugly their church's doctrines could become in the hands of a man willing to use God to justify punching and kicking his pregnant wife, they might even have questioned the church enough that I could have escaped its grasp. Had they known that their son-in-law was pounding their daughter senseless—cutting tendons, cracking teeth, choking her—they may well have intervened in spite of their religion. They didn't know any of those things, so they did what all loving parents do: they raised their child to the best of their ability, shielding her from harmful influences, teaching the values they believed in, praying that God would take care of her when she left home.

Years later, after learning what my marriage had become, they were both stunned to find that I had stayed with someone who had treated me so badly. "But why didn't you just leave him?" my mother cried one afternoon, several years after the divorce. "I surely never taught you to put up with something like that!"

My mother was right. She did not teach me to be what I became: a woman who stayed with a husband who beat her. But my parents did give me a strong set of values, and until the morning Jon, Ruthie, and I left Kevin, I strictly honored them: turn the other cheek; be meek and submissive and kind and gentle no matter what; do unto others as you would have them do unto you. Never once did I raise my hand to hit Kevin back—it was against my personal code (and it would've been a really stupid thing to do as well). Nor did I ever intentionally say or do anything to hurt him—not out of love, for that died very early in our marriage, but out of a refusal to give up entirely the dreams of the young girl I once was. I refrained from hurting him or striking back because I was afraid that in the act of retaliation, I would become what I most feared.

There's nothing inherently wrong with the values I gleaned from my parents' religion—the problem was with me: I interpreted the damn things too literally. The morning I left, that all stopped. I turned aside from my wedding vows and youthful dreams and stepped further into gray nothingness. Walked out on my marriage, effectively renouncing God, and turned my back on everything I had ever believed in—except my son and daughter. That day I was tracking nothing at all. We were barely alive, and I did not expect us to survive very long.

"Why didn't you just leave him?" is one of the first questions our society has for battered women. What we don't yet want to face is that there are many excellent reasons for staying with an abusive man—and not one completely positive reason for leaving. When you leave, things almost always get much worse, and sometimes they stay that way for a very long time. Many battered women and their children do what Jon and Ruthie and I have done now for thirteen years. They run and hide and find their lives ripped apart again and again by fear and torment. Others are less fortunate: They wind up dead, killed by the man they left. Circle that horrifying track if you can. And don't forget to tie flagging to the nearest bush.

SEARCH AND RESCUE

SEARCH-AND-RESCUE TRACKERS learn first to follow tracks on the ground one at a time. Since the distance between one footprint and the next remains fairly constant in any individual, the step-by-step method is both reliable and logical. Only after the next track has been sighted can the tracker move forward. Sometimes the process feels painfully slow, yet as skills improve, trackers can move more quickly.

The maxim still remains useful: "Don't leave one footprint until you can see the next one." Ignoring this means you stand an excellent chance of stepping on the very prints you're trying to follow.

In the world of fantasy and Hollywood, this chapter would recount a fast-paced, breathtaking about-face: formerly abused woman tracker uses her newfound skills to find her children, track down her abusive ex-husband, and blow him away in some isolated desert spot. But providing such a comforting ending would require me to tell a string of bald-faced lies about both our situation and the realities that many abused people continually face in this society. Part of that reality for us is that tracking, no matter what it did for me personally, did not help bring my children home. As Ruthie puts it to this day, in a ragged, angry voice, "The truth is Kevin hated us and got tired of having us there."

Another part of our reality is that neither the abuse nor the threats have ever ended: We all still occasionally have nightmares; we regularly get harassing phone calls; we have to be extremely careful where we go, what we do, when we do it, and who we do it with; and because of the many years of close calls, we will never be able to assume that Kevin is finally going to leave us alone.

None of this probably makes much sense to someone who has never been hunted down. To us it not only makes sense, but constitutes the boundaries of our whole world. Our survival, like that of many other formerly abused people, simply cannot be guaranteed. The safety of any moment is always undermined by knowledge we cannot sidestep: No matter how alert we stay, if this man decides to follow through on his threats again, one or all of us may die a brutal death.

Connections pull trackers into someone else's world. Even if we're only there for a brief moment, and never thoroughly immersed, the bond between us and the one we seek is nevertheless real and quite powerful. These connections exist not simply between tracker and tracked, but at all levels of tracking. In striking ways, the nexus of any given footprint includes unmistakable testimony of its attachments to everything else around it, and each faint mark offers subtle insights into the interrelatedness of all living beings. Beetles walk across tennis shoe tracks, flower petals fall into hiking boot prints, raindrops pepper sandal spoor; lug soles land on a tarantula's almost undetectable trail, bare feet stride across soft new grass, and dune buggy wheels rip through fragile desert varnish.

Yet all these examples are rather elemental, for seldom do you find a track with only one or two related signs nearby. Far more commonly, each track is embedded in a whole web of other spoor: from the insinuated signals of groundwater far below the surface and the composition of its soils, to the constantly eroding rocks and pebbles scattered over or partially buried in that veneer; from the often conspicuous human footprint or tire track, to the many nearly imperceptible traces left by insects, birds, lizards, or small mammals; from the signs of rainfall, dew, heavy or light winds, to the brands left by an extended drought or flash flood or earthquake. No aspect of one existence goes untouched by any other, but we seldom realize just how tightly connected we are to everything else that exists alongside us.

Tracking is routinely an extended, practical meditation on precisely that: the connections between humans and the natural world that surrounds us.

I left the desert I love determined to get an anthropology degree even if it meant Ruthie and I had to live in a big, smoggy city for a while. Frank was transferred to the Rockies, and our home in the desert stood empty for several weeks. (Empty, that is, except for a family of field mice who moved in while the movers were packing our furniture into their van.) By the time the house's new human residents had unloaded their furniture and discovered the field mice ensconced in their new bathtub, I had developed a chronic cough which eventually became asthmatic, and Ruthie had acquired a seemingly permanent scowl: She missed her chuckwalla and primrose friends, and no amount of "citified fun" (plays, parks, movies, and shopping) could supplant her memories of her desert companions. We both missed the emptiness of the desert, and though learning to share our one rented room was an adventure, it was also hard—especially on Ruthie. She made herself a small "nest" behind the bookshelf and called it her "mouse room." Shortly after we moved to the city, Kevin once again called to say that Jon would be coming to live with us permanently.

After nine months of another emotional rollercoaster ride, Kevin sent Jon to California, the children and I moved to a house near the desert, and Frank and I concluded an amicable divorce. Still friends, deeply loyal to one another, we simply could not blend three pieces of one broken family into a unit that included Frank, someone who had no experience of fractured lives. Frank's impulse from the beginning of our marriage was to teach

Kevin a lesson once and for all about how to treat women and kids. But seeing someone like Kevin as trounceable means that you essentially view them as a big bully (not really dangerous, just bothersome), with only intermittent glimpses of their real menace. Frank's closest encounters with Kevin's potential for violence came from fairly sanitized personal contacts, some threatening phone calls, and months of emotional blackmail (which Frank argued I should end by cutting off all contact with both Kevin and my children until they were old enough to escape their father's influence). The few cleaned-up memories I shared with him of specific beatings, his constant exposure to my nightmares and sporadic proximity to Ruthie's or Jon's night terrors or their prosaic observations about their father's abusive behavior never revealed the full horror of what domestic violence actually is.

In the end, even being married to Frank and loving him as much as I knew how, I could never explain to him how fundamentally Kevin's abuse had shaped the children's and my existences. He had to come to that realization on his own, and he did. Nearly a year after Frank and I had divorced, Kevin's anger against us had escalated again and ended in his once more threatening to kill the children and me and, then, in his kidnapping them. After hearing that Jon and Ruthie were gone, Frank drove twelve hundred miles to California. When he learned that Kevin had appeared in court two days earlier at a restraining-order hearing and had used him as a character witness ("her second husband can confirm that she isn't a college student at all, but a prostitute") to insist on a day's unsupervised visitation despite Jon and Ruthie's tearful pleas to the judge not to let their father take them—when he heard that the judge had said he believed the children and me when we told him that Kevin had abused us, but that he also believed children needed to know their biological fathers, so he was ordering a day of unsupervised visitation (with strict orders not to leave the county and with pick-up and delivery of the children at the local sheriff's office)—Frank looked at me as if he'd been punched in the gut and said, "I never really understood all this before."

I once more had no words. Frozen to the core, wanting desperately this time to live, to survive the hell and have my children be safe and happy and unafraid once and for all, I just stood there and shook my head. How could it have happened again? Jon and Ruthie were missing, taken by a man who had said he intended to kill them and me—a man who had vowed "to do it right this time."

I did no tracking at all while Jon and Ruthie were missing, I didn't go to school or work, and I didn't retreat into nature or the desert. For a week I moved through my existence like a sleepwalker: living for some word from my children, some hint of where they might be, some shred of hope that they were still alive. Frank's presence went a long way toward prodding the (belatedly angry) judge to mobilize the legal system on our behalf. And the arrival, one day after the abduction, of sixteen faxes from various professors and college administrators attesting to my honor student standing at a noted private college also didn't hurt. The district attorney's office took the case, assigned their top investigator to it, and for the first time ever, the legal system moved to hold Kevin accountable for something he had done.

One week after the kidnapping, law enforcement officials in another state located Kevin and kept him under surveillance until he left the house alone: After arresting Kevin, though, the officers could not find Jon and Ruthie. While Mom and Frank slept that night, I sat in a corner of my room, staring at the floor, waiting for the phone to ring—too numb to even get into the bed. Over the next few days, my mother and Frank stayed with me, both of them alternating between faltering hope and spiraling despair. I remember trying to be strong for them—that kind of behavior had long ago become my standard response to crises— but I felt my heart had finally come uncoupled from all hope, that I had lost what strength I'd had to share with others. People came by or called to offer help, and many left commenting that I was dealing with the situation "really well," but they all mistook my dazed terror for quiet courage.

Finally one afternoon the phone rang: The D.A. investigator was calling to say she knew where the children were, that she was getting on a plane to go pick them up, and that she would call back as soon as they were actually with her. While Mom and Frank laughed and cried and celebrated, I excused myself, went into the bathroom, and threw up. Not until the next day, when the investigator phoned and put both Jon and Ruthie on the phone to speak to me, did my daze lift. Hope did not return until I heard that she and the children had boarded a plane and taken off, heading home.

Searches are made up of extended spurts of activity interspersed with brief periods of apparent inertia: even trackers have to sleep and eat, and they have to do these things whether somebody is missing or not. As a tracker, I quickly learned to use brief respites to fall asleep instantly under a bush, head on a pack or on the sand, hat over my face and eyes, ears and mind filtering sounds and ignoring most of them for the five or ten minutes I had to rest. These "down times" are absolutely essential for trackers, because they allow one's body and brain and spirit to recover the edge needed to stay alert and on track. Recovery can mean the difference between success and failure on a search.

After Jon and Ruthie returned home, Kevin was allowed to post bail. Over the next six weeks, prior to his hearing, our house was broken into sixteen times. Twice someone picked wet towels up off the bathroom floor, folded them precisely in thirds, and hung them on the towel bar that my children and I made a point of never using. Once he straightened every can in one cabinet, stacking like items together and facing all the labels outward, and left the cabinet door open so its contents would be the first thing we saw on entering the kitchen. All sixteen times, he left a sliding glass door unbolted and standing open exactly six inches.

Three times I found a set of footprints, probably male, size elevens or twelves, leading from the desert into our yard and circling the whole house, stopping at each window. Twice I was able to follow those tracks away from the house, a quarter mile through empty land to a road where the footprints ended in a set of fresh tire tracks. On the advice of the deputy district attorney, we began reporting the break-ins to our local sheriff's department: For the first time in our years of running from Kevin, the police recognized the signs of an abusive ex without my having to mention it to them.

The first officer who responded looked around, took notes, and then asked, "Is there possibly someone in your past who might still be motivated to harm you?"

I was shocked at his intuitiveness and said so. He just shook his head and said, "It's not intuitive—They're training us to deal with these things now, so we have a pretty good idea what we're looking at in this kind of situation."

It was not a solution or a guarantee, but we at least felt we were no longer quite so alone. So when the man in the white car parked on the road a half block from the house and sat there watching us, we no longer ran and hid: We were extremely careful and watched him like hawks, we stayed together and I kept a loaded revolver in a pack strapped to my waist all the time he was there, but otherwise we went about our business as normally as possible.

One morning, as the children were getting ready for school, I looked around to find Ruthie gone. "Jon! Where's your sister?" I called, and Jon came running, saying he hadn't seen her since breakfast.

We both raced frantically through the house, calling Ruthie's name, and finding nothing. As I rushed out the front door, I saw my daughter sitting on a rock near the road, bending over, finger moving through the sand. "Ruthie! Get inside this house this minute!" I yelled, registering that the white car was once again on the road and the driver had his arm propped up on the side window.

Ruthie came running, leaving her backpack by the road, and I hurried her inside, almost sick with fear. "Why on earth would you disappear like that—don't you know it's not safe?!" I yelled into my daughter's face, shaking her by the shoulders. Suddenly I stopped, appalled at what was happening. Ruthie and Jon were both crying, I was shaking, the front door was still open, and for the first time in several weeks I had let my guard down completely: I had no idea where the man from the white car was at that moment. Deadbolting the door, I sank down on the floor, head in my hands, sobbing, begging my daughter to forgive me for scaring her so. Jon and Ruthie came to sit beside me, and I started trying to explain why I was so upset, but Ruthie shushed me. And Jon said, "It's okay, Mom—we understand."

Somehow, I realized, they really did. A calm resignation to our situation began forming in me then, as I sat on the floor talking with my children about specific ways that we could be safe and keep from scaring each other again. They both had good ideas to offer: Ruthie suggested that we come up with a code word to use when we were feeling scared but weren't sure just why; and Jon proposed that since I was a tracker, I could teach them both how to track, so they could help me keep an eye on who had been around the place. We chose a code word and decided to spend the day practicing tracking instead of going to school.

Going out the back door so that the man in the white car couldn't see us, we disappeared into the desert behind our house with picnic lunches and canteens of water. Several hours later, coming back over a hill to the northwest of the house (and road), I pointed out that the white car was gone. We kept following the size eleven lug-soled boot tracks all the way into our backyard to where they stopped beneath the dining room window. Abruptly Ruthie screamed out the new code word and burst into tears. She could not bear the sight of the footprints that close to our home. Jon, too, was shaken and afraid, and the day's tracking—which had seemed so empowering until we reached the window—suddenly felt threatening to all of us.

We went inside, sat down, and made another group decision: no more tracking for a while. Paying attention to footprints would be strictly Mom's job. Ruthie fell asleep on my lap, and Jon lay close by, one hand in mine, the other holding on to his sister's. A few minutes later, he looked up and said, "But Mom—I'll still help watch out for us." And he did. The next evening when the white car reappeared, Jon was the one who noticed it first and suggested that we all go into Ruthie's room, crawl into her closet, turn on the light, and tell funny stories about Mammaw Ruth for a while. Bringing Sam, a quart of ice cream, and a box of cookies along, we did precisely that.

SEARCHER'S DEBRIEFING

NO ONE GOES anywhere without leaving signs. The tracker in each of us always has an opportunity to walk alongside another person, if only for a brief time. My children continue to teach me how to be their mother: they bolster my courage when it's failing; they understand and forgive when I am exhausted and short on hope; they walk beside me every step and help me to believe that we may actually survive the violence that has so irrevocably marked our lives.

Six months after a California judge issued an order forbidding Kevin to contact us directly and suppressing our address and phone number, I received a fellowship to do a year of tracking research in Africa. Jon and Ruthie freely expressed their doubts about the wisdom of the plan, and Ruthie bluntly said she couldn't see how I could possibly need to learn anything else about tracking, but both agreed to come along and see how they liked anthropological fieldwork. Out of the United States, Kevin would be truly unable to reach us, so we could at least have one year to live without fear.

So we packed and repacked, determined to take only what we would be happy to carry in our backpacks. We bought travel guides and language tapes, made passport covers, and turned a lot of the fellowship money into small-denomination travelers' checks. We got our shots, bought antimalarial pills and iodine tablets and sturdy cotton hats, said our good-byes to family and friends, and rode a Greyhound bus across the United States to New York City's LaGuardia Airport.

JANUARY 1992
WESTERN BUSHMANLAND, NAMIBIA
This afternoon I was visiting with a group of Ju/Wasi people under a tree near the water faucet, and happened to notice a very small child sitting on the ground, repeatedly poking her finger into the sand near her leg. She would poke the sand, then wait a few seconds and do it again. Poke and wait. Poke again. Moving a little closer, I could see better what was going on. An ant was attempting to carry a crumb across the sand, and the child was poking her finger into the ground about four inches in front of the ant, which would hesitate momentarily. Then when the ant started to move again, the child would poke the ground again in

almost the same spot. After about three minutes of this, the girl raised her hand and did not poke the ground anymore. Instead she just sat there watching the ant move across the ground until the ant was about two feet away from her. Then she got up and followed and, sitting down a few inches in front of the ant, started the poking process again.

Suddenly the little girl stood up, took a couple steps backward and, from underneath her skirt, started peeing a straight stream of urine about ten inches in front of her—make that *him*self. As the bright yellow liquid splashed all around the ant, the little boy watched and grinned. When the insect righted itself and continued on its way, leaving a partially wet set of tracks for the first few inches of its journey, he watched closely for a few seconds more and then, laughing merrily, toddled off to his mother. No one but myself seemed to have noticed the incident.

There are many places in this world that you can get to by accident: the Kalahari isn't one of them. Our truck had four blowouts between Windhoek and Bushmanland. When we finally passed through the gates of Bushmanland, our last flat tire was many kilometers behind us, but I had the strongest sense that our journey had just begun.

I had come here to study and learn tracking, yet within days of our arrival, our new neighbors had pointed out that my tracking study was deeply irrelevant to both their lives and my own. Although they then proceeded to teach me more about tracking than I'd ever dreamed of learning—a story for another time— the real lessons were about life itself. In the small villages where we lived, people struggled each day to overcome needless illnesses and unjust social conditions. Tuberculosis and malnutrition were as common as physical abuse by authorities. Despite these chilling realities, the villagers who welcomed us into their lives knew how to laugh hard and long even when they were hungry or sick. They taught us to share everything even if we had almost nothing, to listen to even the smallest child with attention and respect. They relentlessly demonstrated how to behave as if a whisper of hope was roughly equivalent to a done deal, and in their communities, we lived for the first time free of the violence of our personal past. For now and always, the little girl who turned out to be a boy stays in my mind and heart, for in his world I—and my children—finally learned that tracking *was* living.

But as we track, we too are being tracked.

For though we had temporarily left behind our own personal violence, and had crossed half the earth and landed in very different cultures than our own, domestic violence marked every place we went. Domestic violence. Such a strangely sanitized choice of descriptive words. We met a young Ju/Wasi woman whose face was battered and bruised and a much older !Kung woman whose face was swollen and blood-crusted. A white Nature Conservation officer had beaten the first woman in the face with his rifle butt, and a local man (who claimed Bushman blood, but looked much more like an Ovambo—very tall and muscular) beat up the tiny old woman because she wouldn't give him her money. Everyone in her small village was angry and upset when I arrived later that day, for the old woman was clearly much loved. Yet they refused to go to the police, because the man who'd done the beating was known to be a friend of the local policemen. To my knowledge, the Nature Conservation officer who battered the other woman's face was not punished or even reprimanded in any way.

We also met the daughter of one of the white farmers one evening. The skin on the right side of her face seemed stretched far too tight, smiling appeared to require a great effort on her part, and her words were halting and at times hard to understand. Halfway through tea and a conversation about religion, her father stopped beside her, gently lifting aside her hair to reveal a jagged, angry scar that almost followed the hairline down to her neck: Her ex-husband had shot her at close range with a .38 caliber revolver. Instead of penetrating her skull at the temple, the bullet had somehow managed to wind its way behind her ear before finally stopping right at her spine. "Can't tell me there's no God," the man said gruffly, sitting down heavily in his chair again.

Nor me.

Domestic violence. Family violence. Intimate violence. By whatever name we wish to label it, the problem belongs to us all. No one escapes its taint, not even those who seem unmarked. We create the most promising human communities when we insist on facing not just the good in ourselves, but also the evil. By learning to really see and listen to one another, by daring to smile and laugh and, yes, cry together, we can overcome what would destroy us. By joining hands, hearts, and efforts, we make human places where a whisper of hope is indeed equivalent to a done deal.

And, with any luck, we can help our daughters and sons learn what *not* to track or imitate from their parents' behavior. For it is no mere cliché to say that "As we track, we too are being tracked." Every action, every inaction, every word, and every silence leaves clear signs for the next generation.

We are home now, all three of us together—Jon, Ruth, and I—living in a small midwestern town, and tracking for us has remained a fundamental part of everyday life. We have brought all the lessons home with us: the community and noncompetitiveness we saw in the Kalahari villages and now see in some of our neighbors; the respect for the wisdom of humans—both young and old—we've glimpsed in many places; a devoted love of stories (Mammaw Ruth's perhaps most of all); and a continuing determination that our lives can only be lived well when they are closely entwined with those of many other species. Sam died last year in the mountains with Frank, but his gentle spirit stays strongly with us, for our house is full of warm-hearted animals: dogs and cats and rabbits, and also mice, spiders, and an occasional string of ants. They keep us company, help us feel safe, and ensure that we stay sane. I still have my awkward ant-avoiding gait and a bad habit of wandering through life with my eyes on the ground. Jon and Ruth haven't picked up either trait yet, but they're betting that Mom will stay that way for life.

FEBRUARY 1996

"Hey, Mom—look!" Ruth called out, motioning for me to hurry across the yard to where she was standing. "Jon!" she added, summoning her brother without an actual command.

Both Jon and I hurried through the deep snow, because Ruth has a knack for seeing some of the tiniest, most easily missed creatures, and we were both curious about what she might have found.

Just as we reached her side, Ruth turned to Jon and asked, "Did you come stand over here by the window this morning when you were shoveling snow?"

Jon was as mystified as I was at her question, but he nodded anyway.

"And did you turn around and look over your shoulder—kind of like this?" Ruth asked, demonstrating what she meant by turning partially toward her left side without moving her feet.

Jon, already chilled and ready to finish shoveling and head inside to the woodstove, said, "What on earth are you talking about?"

I had already looked down at the ground underneath our kitchen windowsill and seen what was motivating Ruth's questions, so when Jon looked at me as if he intended to stalk off without answering his kid sister's question, I said quietly, "Do you remember what you did, Jon?"

After a few moments, he said, "Well, yeah—I was standing here when Eddie called from next door, so I looked over my shoulder at him for a few seconds I guess—"

"A-ha!" Ruthie grinned and gloated. "I *knew* it!" And, pointing to the footprint on the ground, she added, "It's all right there in that track."

Jon leaned over to look at his footprint, shook his head, and then managed a pretend grimace for his sister (who was waiting for his reaction). "Oh no—don't tell me we have *another* tracker in the family!"

Ruth's snowball hit somewhere in the middle of her brother's back as he raced off, sure that his words would have provoked the exact response they did from his little sister. As I watched them go, I realized that we no longer have need for a code word.

Tracking is living. And we are all finally doing both.

ACKNOWLEDGMENTS

Writing may well be solitary work, but it is also an act of community—many layers deep. This book reflects the love and generosity
of an extraordinary group of friends. Deanne Urmy believed that
this story was worth telling long before anyone else did; if she ever
despaired of seeing it in print, she never let on. As an editor, Deanne
has a remarkable gift for being able to reach gently into a writer's
soul and pull out her best efforts without causing the least bit of
damage. Carlisle Rex-Waller brought to the manuscript a light, but
terribly effective copyeditor's hand that improved every sentence it
touched. Bill Cronon and Nan Fey taught me that keeping a stiff upper lip isn't exactly mandatory, and that true strength means letting
your friends be strong for you sometimes without apologizing for
the trouble. Bill has been my advisor, mentor, employer, and friend:
to say he is an inspiration would be the severest kind of understate-
ment. Kris Fossum and Don Brenneis also inspired and challenged
by hiring me to work in a cheerful, collegial basement office whose
most memorable features were lively conversations about theory
and practice carried on beneath a set of gurgling hot steam pipes and
punctuated by our not entirely joking banter about the next earthquake's effect on those noisy tubes (and which one of us would make
it to the top of the stairs first).

Mary Niederehe gave unstintingly of her time and insight and finally succeeded in teaching me the difference between unhealthy selflessness and unhealthy selfishness, and continues to help me find a way to exist somewhere between those two extremes. Greg Summers and Amy Butler managed to make both a hospital stay and graduate school bearable: no small feats for new friends, but enough to link us together long beyond either event. Spinal taps are no fun, but the last one helped me find the finest general physician I've yet met. Dr. Margaret Nelson facilitated not just my return to health so that I could finish this book, but my children's peace of mind—by giving them her home phone number so they'd be able to reach her if their Mom had to go back to the hospital on the weekend.

My parents braved their own fears and histories to raise me to be a good Christian woman, and lived to see the nightmare of that realized goal in my first marriage. Though they remain bitterly disappointed that I still show no signs of becoming their kind of Christian, they gave me much of what it took to survive both my first husband and their God, and I owe them far more than could be repaid in a single lifetime. My little sister grew up while I wasn't paying attention, and her gentle spirit and wicked sense of humor have become a bedrock of my existence; that we have finally found one another remains for me a source of continual delight. I hope one day to find my little brother too. Dennis and Vicki Wilson fed my children and me, gave us a place to sleep, sent no-interest money with no questions asked, shared music, tears, laughter, and even fear without ever once turning their backs on us. No matter how many miles separate us, we always remain next-door neighbors. Jane Skeoch, too, ignoring any risk to herself with all the elegance of the grand southern woman she is, opened her home and heart to us: gave us clothes and food and dishes when we had no money; drove me to the hospital emergency room herself; and for the last dozen years has kept me laughing and believing that one day everything would work out fine.

Craig Patterson shared hikes, hope, hard work, and hellish days until everything did. Melanie Spoo doctored me through meningitis, cheered me through college, and offered unflagging companionship even when we were thousands of miles apart. Flannery Haug walked into our life with her matchless smile and keen intellect, and increased our family by one person and innumerable joys. With great faith and devotion, my son and daughter endured everything—apprehension, empty cupboards, ragged clothing and home haircuts, and a Mom who's been in college for years but still hasn't yet accumulated enough education to understand their jokes. If they are even remotely typical of their generation—the infamous "X" crowd—our world will soon be in much better hands than has ever been the case. Jim Hopkins, soulmate and life partner, helped me heal and believe and begin to sleep without nightmares once again: The day we exchanged vows signaled the start of a truly safe, stable life for us. And then Sollace Mitchell came along and demystified the "other side" of writing, gave me a roadmap to it, walked me through the first disorienting days, and called me a writer confidently enough that even I believed him. I simply cannot imagine having written this book, or having the courage to submit it for publication, without each of these dear friends.

But my community has as many animals in it as people: Sam and Eb, Cody and Tug and Tell and Goose, Gnose and Kit and Zorro, Purna and Manja, Mercutio, Calvin and Hobbes and Laurel and Hardy and Bigotes. Of these well-loved companions, one deserves special mention. For it was Ebenezer who patiently lay on the floor beside my feet every single day, amiably forgoing our walks so I wouldn't miss deadlines and never once complaining (except with an occasional heartfelt groan or two) that my computer was receiving more attention than my dog. Surely somewhere a best friend like Eb inspired the folk saying that has become my daily prayer: Lord, let me become the kind of person my dog already thinks I am.